CHAPTER 19

Undertaking a Direct Foreign Investment

SYNOPSIS

§ 19.01 Foreign Investment in General

§ 19.02 The Opportunities and Risks to the Investor

    [A] The Opportunities
    [B] The Risks
        [1] Political Risk
        [2] Economic and Commercial Risks

§ 19.03 The Opportunities and Risks to the Host Country

    [A] The Opportunities
    [B] The Risks

§ 19.04 The International Framework for Undertaking a Direct Foreign Investment

    [A] In General

§ 19.05 Multilateral and Regional Investment Treaties

    [A] In General
    [B] The European Union
    [C] The North American Free Trade Agreement (NAFTA)
    [D] Foreign Investment and the WTO

§ 19.06 Bilateral Investment Treaties

    [A] Background
    [B] FCN Treaty Provisions on Investments
    [C] Bilateral Investment Treaty Provisions
        [1] Scope of Application
            [a] Form of the Investment
            [b] Economic Area of Activity
            [c] Time of Investment
            [d] Investor's Connection With Contracting State

INTERNATIONAL PLANNING 19–2

    [2] Conditions of Admission of Foreign Investment
    [3] General Standards of Treatment For Investments Once Made
        [a] Fair and Equitable Treatment
        [b] Full Protection and Security
        [c] Protection Against Arbitrary or Discriminatory Measures
        [d] International Law
        [e] Contractual Obligations
        [f] National Treatment
        [g] Most-Favored-Nation Treatment
        [h] Both National Treatment and Most-Favored-Nation Treatment
    [4] Monetary Transfers
    [5] Operational Conditions
    [6] Compensation for Losses from Armed Conflict or Internal Disorder
    [7] Protection Against Dispossession
    [8] Investment Dispute Settlement

§ 19.07 Host Country Investment Laws and Regulations

    [A] In General
    [B] Defining Permitted Investments
    [C] Investment Incentives
    [D] Investment Controls
    [E] Administration of Host Country Investment Laws and Regulations

§ 19.08 Host Country Investment Approvals, Licenses, and Agreements

§ 19.09 Joint Ventures

§ 19.10 Joint Venture Agreements

    [A] Joint Venture Negotiating Process
    [B] The Phases of a Negotiation
        [1] Prenegotiation
            [a] Confidentiality and Exchange of Information Agreements
        [2] Conceptualization
            [a] Letter of Intent or Memorandum of Understanding
        [3] Detail Arrangement
    [C] Recitals
    [D] Organization and Capitalization
    [E] Pre-incorporation Expenses
    [F] Control and Management
    [G] Financial Policies
    [H] Other Obligations and Guarantees
    [I] Auditors and Accounting

UNDERTAKING FOREIGN INVESTMENT 19–3

      [J]   Transfer of Shares
      [K] Dispute Settlement and Applicable Law
      [L]   Termination

§ 19.11   The Legal Form of the Investment Project

      [A] Choosing Between a Branch and a Subsidiary
      [B]   The Organization of the Subsidiary
      [C]   Issues in the Organization of a Foreign Company

§ 19.12   Other Host Country Laws Affecting Foreign Investment

§ 19.13   Debt-To-Equity Conversion: A New Approach to Investment in Developing Countries

      [A]   Background
      [B]   The Types of Conversion Transactions
          [1]   Debt Capitalization Transactions
          [2]   Debt-for-Equity Transactions
          [3]   Debt-for-Local Currency Transactions
      [C]   Reasons for the Development of Debt-Equity Conversions
      [D]   The Structure of Debt-Equity Transactions

§ 19.14   Privatization of Government Assets: Another Mechanism for Foreign Investment

      [A]   Background
      [B]   Reasons and Objectives for Privatization Programs
      [C]   The Legal Basis of Privatization
      [D]   The Process of Privatization
      [E]   Types of Privatization Transactions
          [1]   Public Offering
          [2]   Private Sale of Shares
          [3]   Sale of Government or State Enterprise Assets
          [4]   Reorganization into Component Parts
          [5]   New Private Investment in a State-Owned Enterprise
          [6]   Management and/or Employee Buy-out
          [7]   Leases
          [8]   Management Contracts

§ 19.15   Foreign Investment in Infrastructure: Build-Operate-Transfer (BOT) and Build-Operate-Own (BOO) Arrangements.

      [A]   Background
      [B]   Advantages and Risks of BOT Arrangements
          [1]   For the Host Government
          [2]   For the Project Company
      [C]   Parties to BOT Arrangements
      [D]   Approval Process for BOT Projects
      [E]   Financing of BOT Projects
      [F]   Legal Framework of BOT Arrangements

- [G] **The BOT Concession Agreement**
- [H] **Other Contracts**
    - [1] **Consortium Agreement**
    - [2] **The Project Company**
    - [3] **The Construction Agreement**
    - [4] **Operations and Management Agreement**
    - [5] **Loan Agreements**

§ 19.01 Foreign Investment in General

One of the most significant forms of international business entails the transfer of capital from one country to another for purposes of long-term investment. Foreign investment has traditionally been divided into two basic categories: direct and portfolio. A direct investment establishes or purchases some form of permanent enterprise or facility, such as a factory, mine, plantation, hotel or power station, in whose management the foreign investor will participate. A portfolio investment is one which gives the investor no right to participate in the control and management of the underlying enterprise.[1] Whether an investor has such control, and whether the investment therefore qualifies as direct or portfolio, will depend, of course, on the facts of the individual case; however, for statistical purposes, the United States government classifies an equity investment of ten percent or more as direct.[2]

On the other hand, the International Monetary Fund has a more complex definition of control: "Control of a company in country Y by residents in country X is inferred if (1) 50 percent or more of the voting stock is owned by residents of country X or (2) 25 percent or more of the voting stock is concentrated in the hands of a single shareholder or organized group of holders in X, or (3) residents of X are known in fact to have a controlling voice in the company's policies."[3]

A direct foreign investment may take the form of a wholly-owned branch or subsidiary, or of a joint venture with other investors who may be foreign or host country nationals, private companies or public agencies. Its purpose may be to establish a new enterprise (sometimes called "green field development") or to acquire an existing business or interest therein within the host country. In some cases, the foreign investor may invest alone; in others it may do with a partner, either foreign or local, private or governmental. Portfolio investments—those which do not entail control—can be subdivided into two basic groups:

---

[1] The International Monetary Fund defines direct investment as "investment in enterprises located in one country by effectively controlled by residents of another country." IMF, *Balance of Payments Statistics*, vol. 38, pt. 1, at 10 (1987).

[2] *See* U.S. Dept. of Commerce, Statistical Abstract of the United States 1995 at p.806-807 (115th ed., 1995). *See also* International Investment Survey Act of 1976, 22 U.S.C. § 3102(10).

[3] IMF, *Balance of Payments Statistics*, vol. 38, pt. 1, at 10 (1987).

debt investments, such as loans, bonds and debentures, and equity investments which, by their nature or magnitude, do not give the investor control.

The neat traditional classification described above does not really reflect the complexities of modern forms of international investment. In some cases, for example, one finds that investors in developing countries may have little or no equity in an enterprise but nevertheless control its operation through management agreements or various devices for technology transfer.[4] Indeed, the usual "foreign investment" rarely takes the form of a contribution of equity alone, but also often involves a host of other complex legal arrangements, including loans (both short-term and long-term), exports of equipment and credit arrangements to finance them, licensing agreements, management contracts, and long-term sales and supply arrangements. In most cases a direct foreign investment is not merely a movement of capital, but of persons, organization, technology, know-how, and information as well.[5] The three traditional forms of international business—exporting, licensing, and investing—should by no means be regarded as mutually exclusive modes. As a practical matter, virtually any business undertaking categorized as a "foreign investment" will also involve both export and licensing transactions.

Prior to World War II, the international business activities of U.S. companies, except for extractive industries such as oil, were confined mainly to international trade and to production activities related to trade.[6] Direct foreign investment for the purpose of establishing or acquiring foreign facilities through the transfer of capital abroad was generally limited to a few large companies.[7] After the War, an enormous expansion in international investment took place, and American firms led this new trend of establishing production facilities in foreign countries. For example, the total stock of direct foreign investment by U.S. companies amounted to only $7.5 billion in 1929, but had reached $474 billion by 1992.[8] In that year alone, total direct investment abroad made by United States companies and individuals

---

[4] *See* ch. 12, *Technology Exports.*

[5] K. Grewlich, Direct Investment in the OECD Countries 2 (1978).

[6] V. Salera, *Multinational Business* 7 (1969).

[7] A. Lowenfeld, *International Private Investment* 1-2 (1977).

[8] UNCTAD, *World Investment Report 1993 - Transnational Corporations and Integrated International Production* 14 (1993).

exceeded $40 billion. The growth of this phenomenon can be attributed to a variety of factors, including a gradual lowering of the barriers to international movement of capital, the evolution of sophisticated systems for global communications, the development of institutions and agreements that reduced uncertainty and risks in international transactions and investments, and the increased awareness by U.S. business of economic opportunities in foreign countries.

The United States has not been the only country to participate actively in the phenomenon of direct foreign investment. Companies and individuals in both developed and developing countries have played increasing roles in this movement. In 1994, for example, total direct foreign investment from all countries amounted to $233.5 billion, of which the United States accounted for $58.4 billion, the United Kingdom $30 billion, Japan $ 17.9 billion, other European countries $ 80.1 billion, and developing countries $35.7 billion.[9]

According to the United Nations Conference on Trade and Development (UNCTAD), the total stock of foreign direct investment in the world as of 1992 was $1.949 trillion, of which the United States accounted for $474 billion, the United Kingdom for $259 billion, Japan for $251 billion, Germany $186 billion, and France $151 billion.[10]

The increase in direct foreign investment has been accompanied by the growth of the "multinational enterprise" or "transnational corporation," a corporation or a group of corporations with production and marketing facilities in several countries and which in varying degrees pursues a global—rather than a purely national—strategy in conducting its operations.[11] According to the United Nations, the number of transnational corporations in the world at the beginning of the 1990s was nearly 37,000, and they controlled approximately 170,000 affiliates outside their home countries. Of this number, nearly 90% are based in developed countries and 10% originate in the United States.[12] As of the end of 1993, total U.S. investment abroad amounted to

---

[9] Bank for International Settlements, *65th Annual Report (1st April 1994 - 31st March 1995)* 66.

[10] UNCTAD, *World Investment Report 1993* 14 (1993).

[11] *See, e.g.*, Vagts, *The United States of America and the Multinational Enterprise*, in *Nationalism and the Multinational Enterprise: Legal, Economic and Managerial Aspects* 3–4 (H. Hahlo, J. Smith & R. Wright, eds. 1973).

[12] UNCTAD, *World Investment Report 1993—Transnational Corporations and Integrated International Production* 19-20 (1993).

§ 19.01 INTERNATIONAL PLANNING 19–8

$548.644 billion, and income in that same year to U.S. companies from their foreign affiliates totaled $57.621 billion. Of the amount invested, $199.644 billion was allocated to manufacturing operations, $62.409 billion to petroleum, and $155.597 billion to the financial and insurance sectors.[13] On a geographic basis, U.S. investments at the end of 1993 were distributed as follows: 49% ($269.156 billion) was invested in Europe; 18.4% ($101.936 billion) in Latin America; 12.8% ($70.395 billion) in Canada; 16.8% ($92.269 billion) in the Asia Pacific region, and 5.7% ($31.393 billion) in Japan. Among European countries, the United Kingdom, Germany, France and Switzerland are particularly favored sites for U.S. foreign investment. In general, industrialized countries tend to attract the bulk of U.S. investment abroad because of their stable political systems, advanced markets, well-developed communications networks, abundance of skilled manpower, and economic orientation favorable to foreign business.[14]

The prospective foreign investor faces a host of difficult legal, economic, and political issues when he enters this particular area of international business. For purposes of simplicity, one may divide these issues into two basic categories: (1) problems related to undertaking and establishing a direct foreign investment initially; and (2) problems relating to protecting a foreign investment once it is made. The two are closely interrelated because, for one thing, the decision to undertake an investment project will be significantly influenced by the investor's ability to protect it thereafter.

The purpose of this chapter is to examine the principal issues and problems related to *undertaking* a direct investment in a foreign country. It will focus primarily on the laws, regulations, and investment climate of the host country itself. An understanding of the foreign investment process requires an appreciation of the opportunities and risks of foreign investment to *both* the investor *and* the host country; consequently, the present chapter will seek to provide this necessary background before surveying the various types of host country regulatory schemes currently in effect. Thereafter, it will explore the legal issues relating to the organization of investment projects, particularly those taking the form of joint ventures.

---

[13] U. S. Dept of Commerce, *Statistical Abstract of the United States* 1995, at 809 (115th ed., 1995).

[14] *Id.*

Subsequent chapters, notably those on expropriation (Ch. 27), investment insurance (Ch. 28) and dispute settlement (Ch. 30–32), will treat the principal issues related to the protection of a direct foreign investment.

§ 19.02 The Opportunities and Risks to the Investor

[A] The Opportunities

Planning a foreign investment transaction requires a careful analysis of both its anticipated rewards and its risks to the investor. As will be seen, the nature and magnitude of such risks and rewards may differ significantly from those of a domestic investment.

The decision to invest abroad depends essentially on the business strategy of the firm in question.[1] The basic aim of undertaking any investment, of course, is to increase—or at least preserve—the profitability of the firm. The foreign investor may seek to achieve this goal through a variety of strategies, depending on its own particular situation. One study has concluded that foreign investments are normally motivated by one or more of four basic types of strategic considerations: (1) to develop or protect a market in the foreign country in which the investment is to be located; (2) to obtain raw materials, either for export or for further processing and sale in the host country; (3) to take advantage of underpriced factors of production, such as cheap labor or raw materials, in certain developing countries; and (4) to obtain necessary knowledge or access to technology and expertise by establishing an operation in a host country where such technology or expertise is found.[2] The above-mentioned strategic considerations are not mutually exclusive, for two or more of them may influence a given investment decision. For example, the establishment of a shoe manufacturing plant in Egypt may be motivated by both the desire to employ low priced local labor and to develop a new market in the host country.

In general, regardless of the particular strategic objective in question, the impetus to undertake a foreign investment project is often *defensive* in nature: that is, it is done to protect an established market or source of supply that is threatened by competition. For example, a U.S. battery manufacturer with a large export market in Nigeria might feel compelled to establish a battery plant in that country in order to meet the threat of the import of inexpensive Japanese batteries

---

[1] K. Grewlich, Direct Investment in the OECD Countries 13 (1978).

[2] *See generally* D. Eiteman & A. Stonehill, *Multinational Business Finance* 231–233 (2d ed. 1979). Eiteman and Stonehill have thus categorized investors into 4 types: market seekers, raw-material seekers, production-efficiency seekers, and knowledge seekers.

or to counter a competitor's plans to build such a plant itself. On the other hand, some multinational firms using truly global strategies may, according to one commentator, "scan the world for investment opportunities,"[3] thereby using foreign investment as an offensive tactic to obtain foreign benefits that will help them grow or diversify.

Numerous forces may influence the decision to undertake a particular foreign investment. They include the need to meet competition from abroad in the home market, to keep pace with a competing firm which is experiencing success internationally, to find an outlet for technology and machinery which is no longer suitable for use in the home country, to take advantage of imperfections in foreign markets, and to avoid host country tariffs and other policies that inhibit exports to that market. The literature on investor motivation and decision-making is rich, and the attorney advising international investors may find such resources useful in better understanding the strategies and mentality of his clients.[4]

[B] The Risks

While a foreign investment may offer the investor significant opportunities, it may also present serious risks of a nature and magnitude far different from those involved in investment within the United States. Analysts of foreign investment usually categorize such risks as being either political or commercial in nature, and they consider the existence of political risk as the factor which particularly distinguishes a foreign from a U.S. investment.

---

[3] Kindleberger, *The Monopolistic Theory of Direct Foreign Investment*, in *Transnational Corporations and World Order: Readings in International Political Economy* 105 (G. Modelski ed. 1979). *See also* F. Root, *Foreign Market Entry Strategies* 1–26 (1982). For a discussion of global strategy, see S. Robock, K. Simmonds & J. Zwick, *International Business and Multinational Enterprises*, 399–426 (rev. ed. 1977) [hereinafter cited as Robock, Simmonds & Zwick].

[4] *See, e.g.*, Y. Aharoni, *The Foreign Investment Decision Process* (1966); J. Behrman, *Decision Criteria for Foreign Direct Investment in Latin America* (Council of the Americas, 1964); D. Eiteman & A. Stonehill, *supra* n.2, at 231-59, C. Kindleberger, *American Business Abroad: Six Lectures on Direct Investment* 1–36 (1969); S. Lall & P. Streeten, *Foreign Investment, Transnationals and Developing Countries* 16–46 (1977); R. Rodriguez & E. Carter, *International Financial Management* 432–51 (2d ed. 1979); A. Rugman, *International Diversification and the Multinational Enterprise* 3–9 (1979). *See also* bibliographies in Eiteman & Stonehill, *supra*, at 260–63; in Rodriguez & Carter, *supra*, at 452–54.

[1] Political Risk

Foreign investment faces political risks because the foreign investor must submit its assets and property rights to the sovereign jurisdiction of a foreign state, thereby creating the possibility that the foreign sovereign may exercise its political power so as to interfere with the investor's use of those assets and property rights. Such interference usually takes place when the goals of the investor come into conflict with the national aspirations of the host country or its government.[5] While outright confiscation of the investment is the most extreme and most feared form of interference,[6] interference may also take place in numerous other, less severe ways; for example, host country governments might impose price controls on the sale of the enterprise's products, require the employment of local nationals in its management, prevent the convertibility of host country currency into foreign exchange, levy special taxes, or force renegotiation of investment agreements.[7] Political risk also arises from the possibility that the government of the host country may *fail* to act, for example, when it is unable to protect the property of the investor from damage or destruction resulting from civil disturbance, revolt, or revolution. A political risk may materialize in sudden and violent ways, as in the overthrow of a friendly government. But, it may also take place in a gradual fashion as, for example, when the government progressively raises taxes or tightens controls applicable to the foreign investment project. In general, as will be seen in chapter 28, political risks fall into three general categories: a. governmental interference with property and contractual rights; b. governmental action restricting monetary transfer into and out of the host country; and c. injuries to the investment due to war, revolution and civil disturbance.

In deciding whether or not to undertake an international investment, the investor will have to determine the kinds of political risks that the project might face. The nature and magnitude of political risks will vary from country to country. Indeed, within the same country, the nature of the political risk may differ from industry to industry. Thus, in a given country, a foreign petroleum company may face high

---

[5] D. Eiteman & A. Stonehill, *supra* n.2, at 184.

[6] See ch. 27, *Protection of Foreign Investments*, for a more detailed discussion of expropriation.

[7] *See generally* Vagts, Coercion and Foreign Investment Rearrangements, 72 Am. J. Int'l L. 17 (1978).

political risks of expropriation, while a foreign investment project in food processing may face a lower political risk. The international business community has developed a variety of sophisticated techniques to forecast political risk. But while these methods are fairly effective in predicting general political instability within a particular country, they have been less accurate in determining the probability of expropriation or other political interference to a given enterprise within that country. Nonetheless, these techniques may aid the investor and his attorney in analyzing a proposed investment project.[8] It should also be noted that some large multinational corporations and financial institutions employ experts who analyze and forecast political risk as part of the decision-making process.

Having identified the political risks facing a proposed investment—but desiring to undertake the project nonetheless—the wise investor should seek ways and mechanisms for minimizing such risks. To protect himself, the investor may attempt to negotiate special privileges and guarantees with the government of the host country. For example, the investor may try to obtain a guarantee that the central bank will provide sufficient foreign exchange for debt servicing and repatriation of profits. An investor may also seek to avoid the risk of prejudice or "hometown justice" in any of its disputes with the government by obtaining an agreement stating that such controversies will be submitted to impartial international arbitration based in a third country, rather than to the courts of the host country itself. Other techniques for coping with political risks may lead the investor to modify the structure and operation of the project so as to comply, or at least appear to comply, with the goals and policies of the host country. For example, he might place host country nationals in high management positions to create the impression that the operation is not dominated by foreigners. Indeed, to lessen this impression, he might choose to undertake the project as a joint venture with local entrepreneurs or with a host country public enterprise. In addition, the investor may structure the

---

[8] *See, e.g.*, D. Eiteman & A. Stonehill, *Multinational Business Finance* 159–227 (2d ed. 1979); R. Green, *Political Instability as a Determinant of U.S. Foreign Investment* (1972); D. Haendel, *Foreign Investments and the Management of Political Risk* (1979); Robock, Simmonds & Zwick, *supra* n.3, at 288–306; L. Thunell, *Political Risks in International Business: Investment Behavior of Multinational Corporations* (1977); Kobrin, *Political Risk: A Review and Reconsideration*, 10 J. Int'l Bus. Stud. 69 (Spring/Summer 1979); Rummel & Heenan, *How Multinationals Analyze Political Risk*, 56 Harv. Bus. Rev. 67 (January-February, 1978).

operation so that its foreign subsidiary is so dependent upon the parent for technology, components, and other needs that the host country government may hesitate to expropriate or intervene for fear that the parent will cease to supply the subsidiary, thereby rendering it valueless. Finally, the investor may wish to shift the political risk of the project to a third party by securing investment insurance, a topic which is treated at length in Chapter 28 *infra.*

Despite all of these devices, it must be remembered that the host country has sovereignty over the assets placed within its jurisdiction, and therefore has the ability to interfere unilaterally with the use of those assets. Consequently, the wise investor will keep in mind the possibility of the various forms of political risk and seek to mitigate those risks by appropriate planning, both in the organization and the operation of the investment project concerned.

[2] Economic and Commercial Risks

The special risks of foreign investment are not purely political in nature. Investment abroad also has its peculiar economic and commercial risks. At the very outset, the foreign investor in most countries does not have the amount of reliable information that he would have in the United States about the economy in general, special commercial sectors, the market, and other pertinent factors needed to evaluate and plan a specific investment proposal. This lack of available data presents at least two basic problems: (1) it requires the investor to spend additional money and time to obtain the data it needs; and (2) it often forces the U.S. investor to make business decisions on the basis of information that is less reliable and less complete than that which would ordinarily accompany a decision on an investment project in America.

Recognizing this problem, many foreign governments seeking to attract investment have established special organizations and have produced special publications to provide potential investors with information on opportunities in the host country. A list of such organizations with offices in the United States is found in Appendix 19F to this chapter. The reliability and comprehensiveness of the information provided by these offices and their publications varies dramatically from country to country.

Regardless of the nature and extent of information received from official sources, the investor must in every case undertake a thorough feasibility study of the proposed project to determine its long-term profitability. While such studies are expensive to complete, they are a necessary condition precedent to a decision on undertaking an actual investment project in the host country. A good feasibility study can significantly reduce the risks stemming from a lack of information about the country and its economy. Often, in the preliminary phases of an investment project—particularly when the investment takes the form of a joint venture—the nature and method of execution of the feasibility study, as well as the allocation of its costs, will be the subject of a special agreement.[9] Such agreements will normally provide that the actual undertaking of the project is contingent upon a showing by the feasibility study of a satisfactory level of profitability.

Inadequate communications, transportation, and other forms of infrastructure in the host country may also heighten the economic risk of a foreign investment project. For example, the inability of a spinning mill in a developing country to obtain adequate electrical power twenty-four hours a day so as to operate three shifts, or its inability to secure a constant supply of cotton from the hinterland because of an antiquated, narrow-gauge, one-track railway, are but two examples of factors that can destroy the profitability of a project which appeared attractive in its planning stage. Often the investor itself may have to construct infrastructure facilities, such as electrical generating stations and railroads, which in other countries would be provided by the government.

Among the most important risks to be faced by an investment project abroad are those related to foreign exchange.[10] High inflation rates in the host country, as well as fluctuations in the exchange rate of its currency, can severely limit, or even eliminate, the profitability of the project. In addition, the host country may fix the exchange rate at a level that significantly overvalues its currency, thereby increasing project costs with respect to the purchase of local assets and services. Moreover, when the host country government imposes exchange controls and maintains an administered system of foreign exchange allocation, the project faces real risks that it will be unable to pay its foreign obligations, purchase raw materials and components from abroad, or repatriate capital and earnings.[11]

---

[9] *See* Appendix 19A to this chapter.

[10] For a discussion of foreign exchange risk, see §§ 2.05–2.06 *supra*.

[11] *See* Robock, Simmonds & Zwick, *supra* n.3, at 353.

In both developing and industrialized countries, cultural factors may also create economic risks for the investor. The culture of the host country may have an impact on the investment project at every phase of its development—from its negotiation to its organization and operation, and finally to the sale of its products in the local market. In this context, the culture may be defined as "the whole set of social norms and responses that condition a population's behavior."[12] Differences in language, social structure, and values between the home country of the investor and the host country of the project can significantly influence numerous issues, ranging from managing the work force to marketing the product. Failure to heed these cultural differences may result in the failure of the project itself. For example, marketing a product under a trademark using the image of a dog may prove successful in the United States, but might prove unsuccessful in another country where a dog symbolizes misfortune. Similarly, while an American factory worker may oppose any type of paternalistic management practice as a constraint on his individuality, an African factory worker, used to the feeling of solidarity and security of the tribe, may expect—and indeed desire—that management act in a paternalistic way by providing him with guidance, direction and support, even outside the workplace.[13] To mitigate the economic risks caused by cultural differences, the foreign investor must often incur added costs in order to: (1) determine local cultural differences, and then (2) adapt its product, technology, management, and marketing to meet the demands of local customs and culture.

At the same time, it is important to note that culture is not static and that it does change over time. Moreover, the investment project itself may be an agent for cultural change. While certain changes caused by the project may be beneficial, others may be viewed by the local government or population as unwarranted or dangerous interferences in their lives, a view which thereby increases the political risks of the investment. For example, while a modern agricultural scheme may bring desirable improvements in the health, diet, and working conditions of its laborers, it may have a negative effect on the nomadic herdsman who traditionally grazed their cattle on the land now occupied by the project, as well as on the peasant cultivators in the vicinity, who have not been incorporated into the agricultural

---

[12] See id. at 309.

[13] See id. at 313.

scheme. It is therefore important for the investor not only to identify cultural differences and adapt technology and management to them, but also to avoid interfering with those cultural values firmly held by the population.

§ 19.03 The Opportunities and Risks to the Host Country

Like foreign investors, host countries also view foreign investment in terms of its costs and its benefits, its risks and its rewards. It is important for the U.S. investor and its counsel to understand these host country perceptions in order to work effectively with host country laws, regulations and policies affecting foreign investment and to conduct productive negotiations and dealings with local officials.

[A] The Opportunities

Host country governments, as a group, believe that the establishment of foreign investment projects within their territories offer them numerous benefits. Under proper conditions, host governments expect foreign investment to bring to the host countries a combination of resources, skills, and activities that will result in a surplus of output and real income beyond that which goes directly to the investor as profit. This surplus may take the form of one or several particular benefits to the host country.[1] The importance which any single host country attaches to a specific benefit will normally depend on that country's particular situation. For example, an African country with a desperate shortage of foreign exchange may see the principal benefit of foreign investment as a means to improve its foreign currency reserves. On the other hand, an oil-producing state with a balance of payments surplus may invite foreign investment–not to obtain foreign exchange–but rather to obtain needed technology.

Ordinarily, a host country writes its foreign investment laws and policies in such a way as to encourage those special types of projects from which it thinks it will particularly benefit. The limited space available in this section will permit only a brief mention of the various potential benefits of foreign investment to the host country. For example, many foreign investment laws seek to assure that the investor will bring only new resources into the country as part of the project and will not instead merely mobilize existing local resources, for example, by borrowing from local banks. Other benefits to be derived from foreign investment include the creation of new jobs, the transfer of new technology and skills, the creation of improved linkage of the host country to world markets, the development of natural resources,

---

[1] Committee for Economic Development, *Transnational Corporations and Developing Countries: New Policies for a Changing World Economy* 20 (1981) [hereafter cited as Transnational Corporations and Developing Countries].

the strengthening of local industries and production, the improvement of balance of payments–especially when the investment project will yield export earnings–and increased taxes and public revenues resulting from the activities of the enterprise.[2] Host countries often face problems in identifying and evaluating the benefits to be derived from a particular foreign investment project: some effects are indirect and may not be felt for a long time, while others may be difficult to attribute to a foreign investor because domestic conditions or government action may be equally important in creating the effect.[3]

Investment laws and policies often impose "performance requirements" on investment projects to insure that the country will indeed receive the benefits it seeks. Thus, for example, the host country may require a foreign investment project to export a certain percentage of its output or to include a specified amount of local content in its production. Such performance requirements create difficulties and increase costs for the foreign investor. They have been criticized by the U.S. government,[4] and many bilateral investment treaties have urged their reduction or elimination. The concern by investor home countries with regard to performance requirements led to their inclusion in the Uruguay Round Negotiations of the GATT and ultimately to the Agreement on Trade-Related Investment Measures, which binds all WTO members. The Agreement is considered below in the discussion of multilateral investment agreements.[5]

[B] The Risks

Just as foreign investment presents certain risks and costs to the investor so too does it present risks and costs to the host country. U.S. and Western businessmen often claim that foreign investment provides unlimited benefits to the host country and that it costs the host country virtually nothing; consequently, they are surprised and sometimes even outraged when host country governments are reluctant to accept their investment proposals–a reaction viewed by local officials as either naive or disingenuous. It is therefore important that the U.S. lawyer

---

[2] For a discussion of the potential benefits of foreign investment to the host country, see Robock, Simmonds & Zwick, *International Business and Multinational Enterprises*, 173–198 (rev. ed. 1977).

[3] *Transnational Corporations and Developing Countries,* supra n.1, at 21–23

[4] *See International Trade Reporter's U.S. Export Weekly,* (June 8, 1982).

[5] *See also* ch. 3, *International Trade Framework.*

and businessperson understand the perceived risks and costs to the host country so as to formulate proposals and to conduct negotiations in a manner that will lead to acceptance by host government officials and local joint venture partners.

One must not assume that negative attitudes toward foreign investment are found only in developing countries with a socialist orientation. On the contrary, certain industrialized countries have also become concerned about the impact of foreign investment on their economies and societies.

For the host country, the costs of foreign investment may take a variety of forms, and may be economic, political, and social in nature. For example, while a foreign investment project may improve the country's holdings of foreign exchange in the short run, it may in the long run have an adverse impact on balance of payments and drain off national resources through the repatriation of profits, the payment of royalties, and the servicing of foreign debt. Moreover, the presence of foreign capital in the country may be so substantial that the economy, either in reality or appearance, becomes subject to the control of foreigners. Shifting the focus of economic decision-making from local business enterprises to parent corporation headquarters outside the host country may even be viewed as a threat to national independence.[6] Inevitably, the real or imagined consequence of this phenomenon is that the economy—and indeed the country—exists not for the benefit of its own nationals, but for the benefit of foreign interests.

In addition to economic influence, foreign investment may exert political influence in the affairs of the host country. One need not cite the numerous allegations by developing countries against multinational companies which have either attempted to keep certain governments in power and to depose others, to support certain politicians they favored and oppose those they did not. Political interference may also take place in other, more subtle ways, for example, when the foreign investor imports its home country laws and policies in operating the project. Moreover, the foreign investment project may thwart the policies of the host country. For example, a host country pursuing a policy of social and economic equality for its people may discover

---

[6] Rotstein, *The Multinational Corporation in the Political Economy—A Matter of National Survival*, in *Nationalism and the Multinational Enterprise: Legal, Economic and Managerial Aspects* 187 (H. Hahlo, J. Smith & R. Wright, eds. 1973).

that foreign investment will create a privileged class of its nationals who work for, or are in some way associated with, foreign investors and foreign investment projects. Most host countries are aware of the potential political risks posed by foreign investment in their territories, and their concern may be manifested in negotiations and dealings with the investor.

Host country governments perceive additional risks in that the foreign project, instead of fostering and strengthening local enterprise, may actually stultify local business through destructive competition. Such competition is, of course, obvious when the foreign investment project operates in the same area of economic activity as an existing local enterprise; for instance, a foreign investor's battery plant might compete with a local battery plant in the local market. The foreign investor, often equipped with superior financial and technological resources, as well as with special privileges granted by the government itself, may easily dominate the local manufacturer of similar products. But the destructive effects may also be felt even when the foreign investor and local manufacturers operate in totally different economic domains. For example, a local foundry in a developing country may discover that it is in competition with a foreign battery manufacturing project, not for customers, but for human and financial resources in an economy of scarcity. Because of its power and special privileges, the foreign investment project can command foreign exchange for needed imports and can pay high salaries to attract skilled workers in a way that the foundry cannot. In countries where public sector corporations[7] play an important role in the economy and follow policies of social welfare, rather than policies of pure maximization of profit, host country officials fear that such public entities will become increasingly unprofitable and ultimately depend on government subsidies as they compete with foreign enterprises who are freed of such social obligations and have superior financial and technological capabilities.

While foreign investment may transfer needed technology to the host country, it also presents the risk that such technology will be inappropriate to the conditions prevailing in the country and harmful to the environment. For example, the methods used by a foreign investor to conduct logging operations in a tropical country may

---

[7] See § 1.04[C] supra.

encourage erosion in the areas worked. Or, the introduction of capital-intensive technology, such as a highly-mechanized factory in an area of great unemployment, may result in further labor displacement and local resentment. In addition, the foreign investment project, accompanied by a sizeable presence of foreigners, may have an adverse impact upon the society. It may disrupt established values, change living patterns and erode traditional authority. Thus, a large touristic complex in a small developing country may lead to undesirable behavior among local youths, and factories producing certain types of luxury consumer goods may create undesirable consumption patterns in the society as a whole.

Few countries view foreign investment as an unmixed blessing. Most recognize that it has its benefits and its costs. As a result, host country governments, while seeking to attract capital from abroad, will ordinarily attempt to maximize its benefits and minimize its costs to the society through a variety of devices. Indeed, that is the primary objective of the investment legislation and regulatory schemes prevailing in most countries throughout the world. The elements of such laws and regulations are discussed in detail in section 19.07, *infra*.

§ 19.04 The International Framework for Undertaking a Direct Foreign Investment

[A] In General

As indicated above, planning a foreign investment project normally creates concern about two sets of legal issues:

1. those relating to undertaking the investment in the first place, and
2. those relating to the protection of the investment once it is made.

The law of the host country is naturally the primary source of rules and principles with respect to both sets of issues; however, before considering this national legislation, it is important to explore the extent to which international law is applicable in undertaking a foreign investment. International law consists essentially of customary rules of international law, general principles of law common to the world's legal systems, and international treaties and agreements.

The great growth of foreign investment during the twentieth century has not been accompanied by an equal development in international law on the subject. Few rules of customary international law or general principles of law evolved to govern the field of foreign investment. As late as 1970, the International Court of Justice in the well-known *Barcelona Traction Case* would state:

> Considering the important developments of the last half-century, the growth of foreign investments and the expansion of international activities of corporations, in particular of holding companies, which are often multinational, and considering the way in which the economic interests of states have proliferated, it may at first sight appear surprising that the evolution of law has not gone further and that no generally accepted rules in the matter have crystallized on the international plane.[1] Customary international law offers few binding rules on undertaking a direct foreign investment. Generally speaking, the ability of a U.S. business to undertake an investment project in a foreign country is subject exclusively to the sovereignty of the host country. It is well settled in international law that a state has the right to control the movement of capital into its territory, to regulate all matters pertaining to the acquisition and transfer of

---

[1] Barcelona Traction Company (Belg. v. Spain), 1970 I.C.J. 3, 46-47.

property within its national boundaries, to determine the conditions for the exercise of economic activity by natural or legal persons, and to control the entry and activities of aliens.[2] Thus, unless there is a specific treaty to the contrary, a foreign investor requires the approval of the host country government to undertake an investment project and has no right to make such investment on the basis of customary international law. Customary international law also has few generally accepted, clear rules governing the operation and protection of direct investments abroad.

In the face of this void in customary international law, capital-exporting nations have undertaken efforts to create international rules through treaties that would facilitate and protect the foreign investments of their nationals and companies. These efforts have taken place at both the bilateral and multi-lateral levels, which though separate, tended to inform and reinforce one another. This chapter will first examine the applicability of multilateral treaties to foreign investment and then will consider the role of bilateral treaties.

---

[2] A. Fatouros, *Government Guarantees to Foreign Investors* 40–41 (1962).

§ 19.05 Multilateral and Regional Investment Treaties

[A] In General

The growth of foreign investment after World War II was accompanied by various efforts, both official and non-governmental, to prepare multilateral conventions governing foreign investment exclusively. These included the International Chamber of Commerce's International Code of Fair Treatment of Foreign Investment (1949), the International Convention for the Mutual Protection of Private Property Rights in Foreign Countries (1957), a private effort known as the Abs-Shawcross Convention, and the OECD Draft Convention on the Protection of Foreign Property (1967), among others.[1] Although none of these efforts was ever adopted, they did inform and influence later developments.

Despite efforts since World War II to facilitate and liberalize the movement of capital among the nations of the world, few treaties have succeeded in modifying the principle of national sovereignty over the entry of foreign investments. Thus far, the nations of the world have failed to establish a multilateral framework of international rules to encourage investment across national boundaries, similar to the General Agreement on Tariffs and Trade,[2] which created a multilateral framework to facilitate international trade. International law has traditionally recognized capital controls as an area in which national governments have authority to act, and even the Articles of Agreement of the International Monetary Fund provide that member states may exercise whatever controls are necessary to regulate capital movements.[3] Although various states at different times since World War II have undertaken multilateral efforts to liberalize the movement of capital, most of these attempts have failed to receive broad acceptance or are still in the preparatory stage. Consequently, they have done little to disturb the basic principle that a state has sovereignty to control the entry and establishment of foreign investments within its territory.[4]

---

[1] For a survey of the various multilateral efforts to prepare treaties on foreign investment, see F. Tschofen, *Multilateral Approaches to the Treatment of Foreign Investment*, 7 ICSID Review - Foreign Investment Law Journal 384, 385-86 (1992).

[2] *See* § 3.05, *supra*.

[3] Art. VI, § 3, IMF, Articles of Agreement—Second Amendment (1976). *See* § 2.04[B] and Appendix 2A *supra*.

[4] Note also that two comprehensive multilateral codes relating to foreign direct investment expressly reserve to host countries the right to control entry of foreign

One multilateral effort is worthy of note: the Code of Liberalization of Capital Movements,[5] adopted originally in 1961 by the Council of the Organization for Economic Co-operation and Development (OECD) and subjected to several amendments since that time. By virtue of this agreement, the members of the OECD, a group consisting primarily of industrialized states, agree progressively to abolish among one another restrictions on the movement of capital to the extent necessary for effective economic cooperation. Among the specific liberalization measures to be taken, Article 2 of the Code provides that members are to grant any authorization required for the conclusion or execution of investments by nonresidents in the country concerned by means of: (1) the creation or extension of a wholly-owned enterprise, subsidiary, or branch, or by the acquisition or full ownership of an existing enterprise; (2) the participation in a new or existing enterprise; and (3) long-term loans of 5 years or more. Thus, in addition to affording various protective provisions to foreign investments, the Code seeks to allow nationals of one member country to undertake freely investments in another member country.

The Code has not yet fostered the high degree of capital movement among the OECD countries, for it has not received unanimous acceptance by all OECD members. Those that have accepted it have done so only with significant reservations.[6] Indeed, their restrictions are so broad and so numerous that most OECD members have effectively retained the right to authorize or prevent the entry of a foreign investment within their territories. Nonetheless the Code does constitute a basis for further negotiation on principles to allow the free flow of investments among OECD member states.

---

investment. *See, e.g.*, Organization for Economic Co-operation and Development (OECD), *Declaration by the Governments of OECD Member Countries and Decisions of the OECD Council on Guidelines for Multinational Enterprises, National Treatment, International Investment Incentives and Disincentives, Consultation Procedures* 12 (rev. ed. 1979): ". . . this Declaration does not deal with the right of Member countries to regulate the entry of foreign investment or the conditions of establishment of foreign enterprises;" U.N. Economic and Social Council's Commission on Transnational Corporations, *Draft Code of Conduct on Transnational Corporations, Formulations by the Chairman*, U.N. Doc. E/C. 10/AC. 2/8, December 13, 1978: "this Code does not affect the right of countries to regulate the establishment or entry of transnational corporations, including prohibitions or limitations on the extent of foreign presence in specified sectors."

[5] Organization for Economic Co-operation and Development, *Code of Liberalization of Capital Movements (1973, updated ed. 1978).*

[6] *Id.* at Annex B.

Probably the most significant multilateral arrangements modifying the basic principle on national sovereignty over the entry of foreign investment have taken place at the regional level. Of particular note are the Treaty of Rome, which established the European Union(EU) and the Agreement among the United States, Canada, and Mexico creating the North American Free Trade Agreement (NAFTA). A more geographically broad, but functionally more narrow multi-lateral treaty is the Agreement on Trade-Related Investment Measures which emerged from the Uruguay Round GATT Negotiation and which binds all members of the World Trade Organization. The investment provisions of each of these multilateral treaties are considered below.

[B] The European Union

The Treaty of Rome, which created the European Common Market that is known today as the European Union, provides that there shall be freedom of capital movements (article 67)[7] and freedom of establishment (article 52)[8] among the member states. Under the Treaty, "freedom of establishment" has two fundamental aspects: (1) the freedom of a national or company of one member state to undertake unsalaried business activities in the territory of another state; and (2) the freedom of such national or company to organize and manage its enterprises in another member state on the same basis as nationals of the host state.[9] Thus, in order to establish a common market with the free movement of commerce and capital, the member states, by virtue of the Treaty of Rome and subsequent EU directives, have abandoned, at least as to each other, the exclusive right to control the entry of investments in each other's territory.

Freedom of establishment in the EU is extended to all those companies having an "existing economic link"[10] with a member state, regardless of the nationality or residence of investors or shareholders. Once such a link exists, the company may establish itself in any EEC member state. The relevance of these EEC provisions to an American

---

[7] *See generally* 1 Common Mkt. Rep. (CCH) ¶¶ 1602–1782.

[8] *See generally id.* at ¶¶ 1302–1495. See especially ¶ 1302.21 for an analysis of the relationship of the capital movement provisions and the freedom of establishment provisions.

[9] E. Stein, *Harmonization of European Company Laws* 26 (1971).

[10] *See* Lang, *The Right of Establishment of Companies and Free Movement of Capital in the European Economic Community*, in *International Trade, Investment, and Organization* 298 (W. LaFave & P. Hay, eds. 1967).

business is, of course, that a U.S. enterprise with such a link to one EU member country may take advantage of the freedoms of capital movement and establishment throughout the whole Union. For example, if an American company organizes a French subsidiary under French law and establishes it in France, it may use the subsidiary freely to undertake investments in all other member states of the Common Market.[11]

[C] The North American Free Trade Agreement (NAFTA)

On December 17, 1992, the United States, Canada and Mexico signed the North American Free Trade Agreement (NAFTA)[12] to put in place the legal structure for one of the largest free trade areas in the world, a free trade area with over 360 million consumers and $6 trillion in annual output. A year later Congress enacted the North American Free Trade Agreement Implementation Act to approve this treaty and give a legislative basis for its enforcement.[13] Although the agreement establishes the international legal framework for trade and investment among the three countries, the U.S. implementing legislation clearly states that no provision of the Agreement, or any application thereof, shall have any effect if it is inconsistent with any law of the United States.[14]

Despite the omission of the word "investment" from its title, the North American Free Trade Agreement governs both trade *and* investment among its three members, Canada, Mexico and the United States. In effect, Chapter Eleven of NAFTA, entitled "Investment," constitutes an investment treaty among the three countries.[15] In order to facilitate the flow of capital within the NAFTA area, Chapter Eleven seeks 1) to reduce or remove barriers to investment in one country by investors of another member country, 2) to create a secure investment climate by specifying clear rules concerning the treatment

---

[11] E. Stein, *supra* n.9, at 34; *see generally id.*

[12] North American Free Trade Agreement Between the Government of the United States of America, the Government of Canada and the Government of the United Mexican States (U.S. Government Printing Office, 1993) [hereinafter NAFTA].

[13] North American Free Trade Agreement Implementation Act, Pub. L. No. 103-182, 107 Stat. 2057, 19 U.S.C. §§ 3301–3473.

[14] *Id.*

[15] NAFTA, Arts. 1101-1139. *See generally,* Price, Daniel M., *An Overview of the NAFTA Investment Chapter: Substantive Rules and Investor-State Dispute Settlement,* 27 The International Lawyer 727-736.

to which NAFTA investors and their investments are entitled, and 3)to provide a fair means for the settlement of disputes between a NAFTA investor and the host country. Section A of the chapter contains provisions on the establishment and treatment of investment, and Section B governs the dispute settlement. In addition, the Chapter contains seven annexes for each member country, stating the various exceptions to Chapter Eleven's general principles, that each state plans to maintain.[16] The scope of application of the NAFTA's investment chapter are to be found in the definitions of "investor" and "investment." An investor is defined to include a "national or enterprise of a Party (i.e. a NAFTA member country) that seeks to make, is making or has made an investment."[17] An "enterprise" of a Party includes all forms of business entities constituted or organized under the laws of the Party. Article 1139 defines the concept of "investment" very broadly to include a wide range of financial and ownership interests in an enterprise. Thus, the coverage of the NAFTA rules on investment are intended to be very extensive indeed.

Key investment provisions to facilitate the flow of capital and the making of investments are to be found in Articles 1102 and 1103 which guarantee to investors and investments of other member countries national treatment or most favored nation treatment (whichever is the more favorable) with respect to the "establishment, acquisition, expansion, management, conduct, operation and sale or other disposition of investments." This principle means that, unless there are specific exceptions to the contrary in the Annexes, a NAFTA government may not treat investors and investments from another NAFTA country less favorably than its treats its own nationals and enterprises. Nor may it treat the investors and investments from another NAFTA country less favorably than its treats investments from any other country. Thus, in the absence of specific exceptions, a member country may not impose special exclusions, requirements, and conditions on investors and investments from other NAFTA countries that it does not impose on its own nationals or on other foreign investors.

Host countries often condition the entry of a foreign investment on the agreement by the investor to accept certain "performance requirements", commitments that the investment will perform in particular

---

[16] *See generally*, Rugman, Alan M. (ed.), Foreign Investment and NAFTA (1994).
[17] NAFTA, Article 1139.

ways, such as by exporting a fixed amount of its production or including a minimum amount of local content in is manufacturing processes. Such requirements distort trade and interfere with the autonomy of investors to manage their enterprise is the most economically efficient way. Article 1106 of NAFTA specifically prohibits a host country from imposing any specified performance requirements on an investment undertaken not only by an investor of a NAFTA country (including investors of the host country) but of other foreign investors as well in connection with the establishment, acquisition, expansion, management, conduct, or operation of any investment. The listed prohibited performance requirements include requirements to export a given level of goods or services, to achieve a given level of domestic content, to purchase, use or accord preference to goods produced or service or services provided in he host country, to transfer technology or other proprietary knowledge to a person in the host country, or to act as exclusive supplier of the goods it produces or services it provides to a specific region or world market. In addition, paragraph 3 of Article 1106 prohibits a host country from conditioning the grant of an incentive or benefit in connection with an investment in its territory on any of the following four specified requirements:1) to achieve a given level or percentage of domestic content, 2) to purchase, use or accord preference to gods produced in its territory or to purchase goods from producers in its territory; 3) to relate in any way the volume or value of imports to the volume or value of exports or to the amount of foreign exchange inflows associated with such investment; and 4) to restrict sales of goods or services in its territory that such investment produces or provides relating such sales in any way to the volume or value of its exports or foreign exchange earnings.

Host country restrictions on an investment's ability to make payments abroad are yet another mechanism to restrict and control investment, since the ability to make such payments is usually basic to the efficient and profitable operation of the enterprise. The right to make such payments, known generally as "transfers" are a subject dealt with in most investment treaties, and Chapter Eleven of NAFTA is no exception. Article 1109 requires each member country to permit all transfers relating to an investment by an investor of another NAFTA country to be made freely, without delay, and in freely usable currency at the market exchange rate prevailing on the date of transfer with respect to spot transactions. Transfer are defined to "include" the transfers of profits, dividends, interest, royalty payments, management fees, proceeds from the sale of the investment and payments made under a contract, among others.

In addition to the above mentioned standards of treatment, the NAFTA chapter on investment requires each country to accord investments from other member countries minimum treatment required by international law, including fair and equitable treatment and full protection and security.[18] Moreover, it establishes a highly specific and detailed standard of treatment concerning expropriation of an investment and the resulting compensation that a host country is required to pay an expropriated investor. Article 1110 states the general rule on expropriation:

> No party may directly of indirectly nationalize or expropriate an investment of an investor of another Party in its territory or take a measure tantamount to nationalization or expropriation of such an investment ("expropriation"), except:
>
> (a) for a public purpose;
>
> (b) on a non-discriminatory basis:
>
> (c) in accordance with due process of law and Article 1105(1);
>
> (d) on payment of compensation in accordance with paragraphs 2 through 6.

It should be noted that Mexico had traditionally resisted this standard in its relations with the United States; consequently, it acceptance of the investment chapter of NAFTA marks a major change of policy.[19] With regard to the standard of compensation, NAFTA requires the expropriating state to pay compensation equivalent to the fair marker value of the expropriated investment immediately before the expropriation took place, to include interest from the date of expropriation, to make the payment without delay in fully realizable and freely transferable currency.[20] In the event that a host country and an expropriated investor are unable to reach an agreement on compensation, NAFTA provides for mandatory dispute resolution through international arbitration.

---

[18] NAFTA, Article 1105.

[19] On this point, see Levy, Tali, *NAFTA's Provision for Compensation in the Event of Expropriation: A Reassessment of the Prompt, Adequate and Effective" Standard*, 31 Standard Journal of International Law 423-453 (1995).

[20] NAFTA, Article 1110, para. 2.

The provisions of NAFTA investment dispute settlement are considered in Chapter 27 on the protection of foreign investments.

[D] Foreign Investment and the WTO

On January 1, 1995, a new international legal framework for trade was established with the creation of the World Trade Organization (WTO) and the entry into force of a complex and broad set of legal principles governing trading relations among nations. This new framework was the result of nearly eight years of negotiations involving 125 nations in the "Uruguay Round" of negotiations among the members of the General Agreement on Tariffs and Trade. Launched at Punta del Este, Uruguay in September 1986, negotiations continued until April 15, 1994 when the Final Act embodying the various agreement negotiated was signed in Marrakesh, Morocco.[21]

The United States approved the Uruguay Round Agreements and enacted the necessary implementing legislation in December 1994 with the passage of the Uruguay Round Agreements Act.[22] One of the treaties concluded in the Uruguay Round affects foreign investment. It is the Agreement on Trade-Related Investment Measures. Although the WTO and its predecessor, the GATT, were established to encourage free trade, the Declaration launching the Uruguay Round of Trade Negotiations in 1986 recognized that ceratin measures imposed by governments in connection with investments had restrictive and distorting effects on trade. It was therefore decided to include them on the Uruguay Round Agenda in an effort to reach an agreement that would limit their use. For the most part such measures fall into the category of "performance requirements",—requirements imposed by host country governments as a condition for allowing the investment that the resulting enterprise operate or "perform" in a particular way. It is to be noted that the NAFTA also seeks to eliminate performance requirements.

The resulting Agreement on Trade-Related Investment Measures prohibits all WTO members from applying any trade-related

---

[21] Office of the U.S. Trade Representative, Final Act Embodying the Results of the Uruguay Round of Multilateral Trade Negotiations (Washington, D.C.: U.S. Government Printing Office, 1994); reprinted in 33 Int'l Legal Materials 1125 (1994). For a detailed discussion of the WTO, see *supra* § 3.05 The World Trade Organization and The Uruguay Round Agreements

[22] Pub. L. 103-465, December 8, 1994, 108 Stat 4809, codified at 19 U.C.S. ss.3501 et seq. For legislative history, see 1994 U.S. Code Cong. and Adm. News, p.3773.

investment measure (TRIM) that is in consistent with Article III of the GATT on national treatment or Article XI prohibiting quantitative restrictions on imports. Since GATT Article III requires a WTO member country to treat an import, once customs duties have been paid and other formalities completed, like national goods, to restrict an investment project's ability to use those goods is in effect to deny them national treatment. Similarly, to impose on an investment project a local content performance requirement so that it may not use imported goods in excess of a certain amount is in effect to impose a prohibited quantitative restriction on imports in violation of the GATT's Article XI.

The Annex to the Agreement contains an illustrative list of prohibited TRIMs. A TRIM is prohibited whether its is made mandatory by law or regulation or whether its is made a condition to obtaining an advantage or benefit. Illustrative TRIMs that are inconsistent with GATT Article III are those which require the purchase or use by an enterprise of products of domestic origin or from any domestic source or those which require an enterprise's purchase or use of imported products be limited to an amount related to the volume or value of local products that it exports. Examples of TRIMs that are inconsistent with Article XI of the GATT are those which restrict the importation by an enterprise of products used in or related to its local production, which restrict the importation by an enterprise of products used in or related to its local production by restricting its access to foreign exchange to an amount related to the foreign exchange inflows attributable to the enterprise, or which restrict the exportation or sale for export by an enterprise of products.

Recognizing that TRIMs have become a basic part of most country's regulatory systems, the Agreement on Trade-Related Investment Measures provides for a transitional period during which TRIMS are to be phased out. Developed countries have two years to eliminate TRIMs, developing countries have five years, and least-developed countries seven years. Moreover, all countries are to notify the WTO of TRIMS that they are applying which do not conform to the Agreement.

Although the functional scope of this multilateral treaty is narrow, it may become a first step in the elaboration of a more broad treaty on foreign investment.

§ 19.06 Bilateral Investment Treaties

[A] Background

Throughout its history, the United States, like many other capital-exporting states, has entered into numerous bilateral treaties whose provisions may have some application to direct investments undertaken by U.S. nationals abroad. Prior to World War I, these agreements, which are most commonly known as "Treaties of Friendship, Commerce and Navigation," sought to facilitate trade and shipping with the country concerned.[1] After that war, however, they increasingly dealt with U.S. investment abroad[2] by securing agreements with potential host countries on the treatment to be accorded U.S. nationals in their territory with respect to the establishment of American businesses, the entry of other types of U.S. investments, the protection of foreign investments from arbitrary or discriminatory action, and the mechanisms for settlement of any investment disputes.

After World War II, with the great expansion in foreign investment by American corporations, the United States government undertook a program to conclude a network of bilateral treaties of friendship, commerce and navigation which, in addition to other commercial matters, specifically sought to facilitate and protect U.S. direct foreign investments.[3] From 1946 until 1966, the U.S. signed approximately 22 such treaties;[4] however, this effort lost momentum by the early 1970s, as developing countries became more skeptical of the benefits which they might derive from unregulated foreign investment.[5]

---

[1] For a history of U.S. Treaties of Friendship, Commerce and Navigation, *see generally* Walker, *Modern Treaties of Friendship, Commerce and Navigation*, 42 Minn. L. Rev. 805 (1958). *See also* R. Wilson, *United States Commercial Treaties and International Law* (1960).

[2] Norton, *The Renegotiability of United States Bilateral Commercial Treaties with the Member States of the European Economic Community*, 8 Tex. Int'l L. Rev. 299, 306-307 (1973).

[3] For a discussion by the U.S. Supreme Court of the history of U.S. bilateral treaties, see Sumitomo Shoji America, Inc. v. Avagliano, 457 U.S. 176 (1982).

[4] Note, *Developing a Model Bilateral Investment Treaty*, 14 L. & Pol. Int'l Bus. 273, 276 (1983). As of 1981, FCN treaties were in force between the United States and approximately 50 foreign countries. For a compilation prepared by the State Department of FCN treaties in force see 20 Int'l Legal Materials 565 (1981).

[5] J. Salacuse, *Towards a New Treaty Framework for Direct Foreign Investment*, 50 J. Air L. & Com. 969, 900-991 (1985).

Consequently, they were unwilling to make the types of guarantees requested by the U.S. government to protect and encourage investments by American nationals and companies.

In the early 1960s, European capital-exporting states began their own treaty programs, which unlike the U.S. approach, dealt *exclusively* with foreign investment and sought to create a basic legal framework to govern investments by nationals of one signatory country in the territory of the other. These agreements, known as bilateral investment treaties (BIT's), gained the approval of numerous developing countries. By the beginning of 1980, the European countries had concluded approximately 150 such agreements with a broad array of developing nations.[6] The modern bilateral treaty movement was thus born.[7] Germany, which had lost all of its foreign investments as a result of its defeat in World War II, took the lead in this new phase of bilateral treaty-making. Beginning with the first such agreement with Pakistan in 1959, Germany proceeded to negotiate similar investment treaties with countries throughout the developing world, and today it remains the leader numerically, having concluded 77 BITs by 1991.[8] Switzerland, France, the United Kingdom, the Netherlands and Belgium followed in relatively short order. The reason for the greater success of the European programs is not completely clear, but it may lie in the fact that the European countries were less demanding than were the Americans with respect to guarantees on free convertibility of local currency, the abolition of performance requirements, the protection against expropriation, and the elimination of investment screening procedures.[9] Moreover, the special relationship between former colonial powers in Europe and their erstwhile colonies may have predisposed some newly independent countries to conclude investment treaties with their previous colonial rulers, particularly if they believed that a BIT was a condition for foreign aid.

---

[6] ICC, *Bilateral Treaties for International Investment* (1980).

[7] *See generally*, Salacuse, Jeswald W., *BIT By BIT: The Growth of Bilateral Investment Treaties and Their Impact on Foreign Investment In Developing Countries*, 29 The Int'l Lawyer 655-675 (1990).

[8] UNCTC, *Bilateral Investment Treaties 1959-1991* p.2 (1992).

[9] Coughlin, *The U.S. Bilateral Investment Treaty: An Answer to Performance Requirements?*, in Regulating the Multinational Enterprise: National and International Challenges, 129, 136-137 (Fisher & Turner eds. 1983). *See also* K. Scott Gudgeon, *United States Bilateral Investment Treaties: Comments on Their Origin, Purposes, and General Treatment Standards*, 4 Int'l Tax & Bus. Law., 105, 110 (1986).

With the inauguration of the Reagan administration in 1981, the United States, encouraged by the experience of the Europeans, also undertook to foster capital flows through its own program of specific bilateral investment treaties. At the International Meeting on Cooperation and Development in October 1981, at Cancun, Mexico, President Reagan stressed the role of private capital in aiding the developing world.[10] Shortly thereafter, to advance its goal, the U.S. government announced its willingness to negotiate bilateral investment treaties, and the Office of the U.S. Trade Representative prepared a prototype BIT for use in negotiations.[11] That prototype was subsequently revised as a result of negotiating experience.[12]

Since preparing the prototype, the U.S. government has been actively engaged in negotiating bilateral investment treaties throughout the developing world. By 1986, it had signed 10 such treaties, and President Reagan transmitted them to the Senate for ratification in that year. Concerns in the Senate about the effect of the treaties on the United States' ability to take action to protect its national security delayed ratification for a time. But ultimately, in late 1988, the Senate approved and President Reagan signed 8 of these 10 treaties with a proviso that "either Party may take all measures necessary to deal with any unusual and extraordinary threat to its national security."[13]

With the debt crisis of 1982 and the increased reluctance of international commercial banks to make loans to developing nations, host countries increasingly liberalized their laws to encourage foreign investment and they also demonstrated increased willingness to enter into bilateral investment treaties in hopes of securing needed capital for development. As a result by July 1997, the United States had signed and ratified twenty-nine BITs, and an additional ten had been signed and were awaiting ratification.[14] As certain non-western countries

---

[10] *See* Note, *Developing a Model Bilateral Investment Treaty*, 15 L. & Pol. Int'l Bus. 273 (1983).

[11] Model Bilateral Investment Treaty Proposed by U.S. Trade Representative, January 11, 1982, reprinted in Export Weekly (BNA) 734 (Mar. 23, 1982). A subsequently modified version appears in Appendix 27D, *infra*.

[12] Revised Model Bilateral Investment Treaty, February 24, 1984, *reprinted in* 20 Export Weekly (BNA) 980 (May 15, 1984).

[13] *Congressional Record-Senate*, Oct. 20, 1988, S 16940. The President signed the eight treaties on December 6, 1988.

[14] As of July 1997, the ratified U.S. bilateral investment treaties were as follows:

(Text continued on page 19-39)

Senegal: Agreement Concerning the Reciprocal Encouragement and Protection of Investment, Dec. 6, 1983, U.S.-Sen., S. Treaty Doc. No. 15, 99th Cong., 2d Sess. (1986) (entered into force Oct. 25, 1990).

Panama: Treaty Concerning the Treatment and Protection of Investments, Oct. 27, 1982, U.S.-Pan., S. Treaty Doc. No. 14, 99th Cong., 2d Sess. (1986) (entered into force May 30, 1991). Reprinted in 21 International Legal Materials 1227 (1982).

Zaire: Treaty Concerning the Reciprocal Encouragement and Protection of Investment, Aug. 3, 1984, U.S.-Zaire, S. Treaty Doc. No. 17, 99th Cong., 2d Sess. (1986) (entered into force July 28, 1989).

Morocco: Treaty Concerning the Encouragement and Reciprocal Protection of Investments, July 22, 1985, U.S.-Morocco, S. Treaty Doc. No. 18, 99th Cong., 2d Sess. (1986) (entered into force May 29, 1991).

Turkey: Treaty Concerning the Reciprocal Encouragement and Protection of Investments, Dec. 3, 1985, U.S.-Turk., S. Treaty Doc. No. 19, 99th Cong., 2d Sess. (1986) (entered into force May 18, 1990). Reprinted in 25 Int'l Legal Materials 85 (1986).

Cameroon: Treaty Concerning the Reciprocal Encouragement and Protection of Investment, Feb. 26, 1986, U.S.-Cameroon, S. Treaty Doc. No. 22, 99th Cong., 2d Sess. (1986) (entered into force Apr. 6, 1989).

Bangladesh: Treaty Concerning the Reciprocal Encouragement and Protection of Investment, Mar. 12, 1986, U.S.-Bangl., S. Treaty Doc. No. 23, 99th Cong., 2d Sess. (1986) (entered into force July 25, 1989).

Egypt: Treaty Concerning the Reciprocal Encouragement and Protection of Investments, Sep. 29, 1982, U.S.-Egypt, S. Treaty Doc. No. 24, 99th Cong., 2d Sess. (1986) (entered into force June 27, 1992); with a Related Exchange of Letters signed Mar. 11,1986. Reprinted in 21 Int'l Legal Materials 927 (1982).

Grenada: Treaty Concerning the Reciprocal Encouragement and Protection of Investment, May 2, 1986, U.S.-Gren., S. Treaty Doc. No. 25, 99th Cong., 2d Sess. (1986) (entered into force Mar. 3, 1989).

Congo: Treaty Concerning the Reciprocal Encouragement and Protection of Investment, Feb. 12, 1990, U.S.-Congo, S. Treaty Doc. No. 1, 102d Cong., 1st Sess. (1991) (entered into force Aug. 13, 1994).

Poland: Treaty Concerning Business and Economic Relations, March 21, 1990, S. Treaty Doc. No. 18, 101st Cong., 2d Sess.(1990) (entered into force Aug. 6,1994); reprinted in 29 Int'l Legal.Materials 1194 (1990).

Tunisia: Treaty Concerning the Reciprocal Encouragement and Protection of Investment, May 15, 1990, U.S.-Tunis., S. Treaty Doc. No. 6, 102d Cong., 1st Sess. (1991) (entered into force Feb. 7, 1993).

Sri Lanka: Treaty Concerning the Encouragement and Reciprocal Protection of Investment, Sep. 20, 1991, U.S.-Sri Lanka, S. Treaty Doc. No. 46, 102d Cong., 2d Sess. (1992) (entered into force May 1, 1993).

Czechoslovakia: Treaty Concerning the Reciprocal Encouragement and Protection of Investment, Oct. 22, 1991, U.S.-Czech., S. Treaty Doc. No. 47, 102d Cong., 2d Sess. (1992) (entered into force Dec. 19, 1992). This treaty entered into force for the Czech Republic and Slovakia as separate states on January 1, 1993.

(Text continued on page 19-39)

Romania: Treaty Concerning the Reciprocal Encouragement and Protection of Investment, May 28, 1992, U.S.-Rom., S. Treaty Doc. No. 36, 102d Cong., 2d Sess. (1992) (entered into force Jan. 15, 1994).

Argentina: Treaty Concerning the Reciprocal Encouragement and Protection of Investment, Nov. 14, 1991, U.S.-Arg., S. Treaty Doc. No. 8, 103d Cong., 1st Sess. (1993) (entered into force Oct. 20, 1994). Reprinted in 31 International Legal Materials 128 (1992).

Bulgaria: Treaty Concerning the Encouragement and Reciprocal Protection of Investment, Sep. 23, 1992, U.S.-Bulg., S. Treaty Doc. No. 9, 103d Cong., 1st Sess. (1993) (entered into force June 2, 1994).

Kazakhstan: Treaty Concerning the Reciprocal Encouragement and Protection of Investment, May 19, 1992, U.S.-Kazakhstan, S. Treaty Doc. No. 11, 103d Cong., 1st Sess. (1993) (entered into force Jan. 12, 1994).

Kyrgyz Republic: Treaty Concerning the Encouragement and Reciprocal Protection of Investment, Jan. 19, 1993, U.S.-Kyrgyz Rep., S. Treaty Doc. No. 12, 103d Cong., 1st Sess. (1993) (entered into force Jan. 12, 1994).

Moldova: Treaty Concerning the Encouragement and Reciprocal Protection of Investment, Apr. 21, 1993, U.S.-Moldova, S. Treaty Doc. No. 13, 103d Cong., 1st Sess. (1993) (entered into force Nov. 25, 1994).

Armenia: Treaty Concerning the Reciprocal Encouragement and Protection of Investment, Sep. 23, 1992, U.S.-Armenia, S. Treaty Doc. No. 11, 103d Cong., 1st Sess. (1993) (entered into force March 29, 1996).

Ecuador: Treaty Concerning the Encouragement and Reciprocal Protection of Investment, Aug. 27, 1993, U.S.-Ecuador, S. Treaty Doc. No. 13, 103d Cong., 1st Sess. (1993) (entered into force May 11, 1997).

Jamaica: Treaty Concerning the Reciprocal Encouragement and Protection of Investment, Feb. 4, 1994, U.S.-Jam., S. Treaty Doc. No. 36, 103d Cong., 2d Sess. (1994) (entered into force March 7, 1997).

Ukraine: Treaty Concerning the Encouragement and Reciprocal Protection of Investment, Mar. 4, 1994, U.S.-Ukraine, S. Treaty Doc. No. 37, 103d Cong., 2d Sess. (1994) (entered into force November 16,1996).

Estonia: Treaty Concerning the Encouragement and Reciprocal Protection of Investment, Apr. 19, 1994, U.S.-Estonia, S. Treaty Doc. No. 38, 103d Cong., 2d Sess. (1994) (entered into force February 16, 1997).

Latvia: Treaty Concerning the Encouragement and Reciprocal Protection of Private Investments, Jan. 13, 1995, U.S.-Latvia, S. Treaty Doc. No. 12, 104th Cong., 1st Sess. (1995) (entered into force December 26, 1996).

Trinidad and Tobago: Treaty Concerning the Encouragement and Reciprocal Protection of Private Investments, Sep. 26, 1994, U.S.-Trin. & Tobago, S. Treaty Doc. No. 14, 104th Cong., 1st Sess. (1995) (entered into force December 26, 1996).

Mongolia: Treaty Concerning the Encouragement and Reciprocal Protection of Private Investments, Oct. 6, 1994, U.S.-Mong., S. Treaty Doc. No. 10, 104th Cong., 1st Sess. (1995) (entered into force January 1, 1997).

began to export capital, they too negotiated bilateral treaties to create a legal framework for their nationals' investments in specific countries. By 1991, Kuwait, for example, which had accumulated capital as a result of a substantial growth in oil revenues, had signed eleven BITs, and Japan had concluded agreements with Egypt, China, and Sri Lanka.[15] Although the usual BIT is between a capital-exporting state and a developing country, occasionally two developing countries or two industrialized countries have also made them. Examples of the former include BITs between Thailand and China, and between Egypt and Morocco, while the most notable example of the latter was the United States-Canada Free Trade Agreement,[16] signed in 1988. One

---

The bilateral investment treaties signed but not ratified by the United states as of July 1997 were as follows:

Haiti: Agreement Concerning the Reciprocal Encouragement and Protection of Investment, Dec. 13, 1983, U.S.-Haiti, S. Treaty Doc. No. 16, 99th Cong., 2d Sess. (1986).

Russian Federation: Treaty Concerning the Encouragement and Reciprocal Protection of Investment, June 17, 1992, U.S.-Russian Fed., S. Treaty Doc. No. 48, 102d Cong., 2d Sess. (1992). Reprinted in 31 International Legal Materials 799 (1992).

Belarus: Treaty Concerning the Encouragement and Reciprocal Protection of Investment, Jan. 15, 1994, U.S.-Belarus, S. Treaty Doc. No. 36, 103d Cong., 2d Sess. (1994).

Georgia: Treaty Concerning the Encouragement and Reciprocal Protection of Private Investments, Mar. 7, 1994, U.S.-Georgia, S. Treaty Doc. No.13, 104th Cong., 1st Sess. (1995).

Albania: Treaty Concerning the Encouragement and Reciprocal Protection of Private Investments, January 11,1995, U.S.-Alb., S. Treaty Doc. No. 19, 104th Cong., 1st Sess. (1995).

Uzbekistan: Treaty Concerning the Encouragement and Reciprocal Protection of Private Investments, December 19, 1994, U.S.-Uzbekistan, S. Treaty Doc. No. 25, 104th Cong., 1st Sess. (1995).

Honduras: Treaty Concerning the Encouragement and Reciprocal Protection of Private Investments, July 1, 1995.

Nicaragua: Treaty Concerning the Encouragement and Reciprocal Protection of Private Investments, July 1, 1995.

Croatia: Treaty Concerning the Encouragement and Reciprocal Protection of Private Investments, July 13, 1996.

Jordan: Treaty Concerning the Encouragement and Reciprocal Protection of Private Investments, July 2, 1997.

[15] UNCTC, *Bilateral Investment Treaties 1959-1991* 15-37 (1992).

[16] United States-Canada Free Trade Agreement, signed Jan. 2, 1988, *reprinted in* 27 Int'l Legal Materials 281 (1988). *See generally* Note, *International Trade,* 29 Harv. Int'l. L.J. 572 (1988).

of its principal objectives was to liberalize significantly conditions for investment between the two counties, and it therefore included provisions [17] in its Chapter Sixteen, which in effect constituted a bilateral investment treaty. Indeed, the provisions of Chapter Sixteen of the treaty covered most of the subjects, such as treatment, transfers, entry, expropriation and disputes, found in the ordinary bilateral investment treaty. Chapter Sixteen bears the unmistakable imprint of the BITs that the United States had negotiated with other countries, and it in turn would influence Chapter Eleven on Investments under the NAFTA.

The late 1980's witnessed a new chapter in the history of the BIT movement with the end of the communist era. The emerging economies of Eastern and Central Europe, as well as certain Asian nations, which had previously been hostile to foreign investment, entered into bilateral investment treaties with industrialized states from whom they hoped to receive capital and technology to advance their development. According to information received by the International Center for Settlement of Investment Disputes, between January 1, 1989 and June 30, 1992, out of 183 BITS signed, 76 included an Eastern or Central European country. Thus the Soviet Union signed bilateral investment treaties with France,[18] the United Kingdom,[19]

Germany,[20] Belgium/Luxembourg,[21] and the Republic of Korea;[22] Hungary concluded a BIT with the United Kingdom;[23]

Poland signed investment treaties with the United States[24] and with

---

[17] *Id.*, Arts. 1601-1611.

[18] Agreement for the Promotion and Reciprocal Protection of Investments, with exchange of Interpretive Letters, July 4, 1989, France-Union of Soviet Socialist Republics, *reprinted in* 29 Int'l Legal Materials 351 (1990).

[19] Agreement for the Promotion and Reciprocal Protection of Investments, April 6, 1989, United Kingdom-U.S.S.R., reprinted in 29 Int'l Legal Materials 366 (1990).

[20] Treaty concerning the Promotion and Reciprocal Protection of Investments, with Protocol, June 13, 1989, *reprinted in* 29 Int'l Legal Materials 351 (1990).

[21] Agreement Concerning the Reciprocal Encouragement and Protection of Investments, February 9, 1989, Belgium/Luxembourg-U.S.S.R., *reprinted in* 29 Int'l Legal Materials 299 (1990).

[22] Agreement for the Promotion and Reciprocal Protection of Investments, December 14, 1990, Korea-U.S.S.R., *reprinted in* 30 Int'l Legal Materials 762 (1991).

[23] Agreement for the Promotion and Reciprocal Protection of Investments, March 9, 1987, United Kingdom-Hungary, U.K. Treaty Series, No.3 (1988) CMD 281.

[24] Treaty Concerning Business and Economic Relations, March 21,1990, United States-Poland, *reprinted in* 29 Int'l Legal Materials 1194 (1990). *See generally*

Germany;[25] and Vietnam concluded a BIT with Australia.[26] More recently, important parts of the world, such as Latin America and India, which had refrained steadfastly from entering into bilateral investment treaties and had demonstrated resistance to foreign investment generally, have shown signs of joining the BIT movement.[27] By 1995, the BIT movement had resulted in a dense network of some seven hundred treaties linking 140 different countries.

The impetus for the flurry of BIT-making activity over the last five decades has been the strong drive by nationals and companies in a growing number of industrialized states to undertake direct foreign investments in developing countries and their consequent need to create a stable international legal framework to facilitate and protect those investments. For these international investors, relying on host country law alone subjected their capital to a variety of risks. Host governments may easily change a law after an investment is made, and host country officials may not always act fairly or impartially toward foreign investors and their enterprises. These considerations proved to be more than theoretical, for the 1960's and 1970's witnessed numerous instances of interference and expropriation by host country governments with foreign investments in their territories.

International law offered foreign investors little effective protection against these risks. Not only did customary international law contain no generally accepted rules on the subject, but it also lacked a binding, impartial mechanism to settle investment disputes between foreign investors and host governments. Moreover, the very nature of the international law governing foreign investment became a matter of serious controversy in the 1960's and 1970's with the demand by developing countries for the establishment of a New International Economic Order. While capital-exporting states asserted that international law imposed an obligation on host countries to accord foreign

---

International Trade: Poland Bilateral Investment Treaty - A Reflection of United States efforts to Shape the Economic Development of Eastern Europe, 32 Harvard Int'l Law Journal 255-264 (1991).

[25] Agreement for the Promotion and Reciprocal Protection of Investment, Poland-Germany, 29 Int'l Legal Materials 1064 (1990).

[26] Agreement on the Reciprocal Promotion and Protection of Investments, March 5, 1991, Australia-Vietnam, 30 Int'l Legal Materials 1064 (1991).

[27] Agreement for the Promotion and Protection of Investments, March 14, 1994, India-United Kingdom, *reprinted in* 34 Int'l Legal Materials 935 (1995); Treaty Concerning the Reciprocal Encouragement and Protection of Investments, November 14, 1991, *reprinted in* 31 Int'l Legal Materials 124 (1992).

investors a minimum standard of protection,[28] many developing countries rejected this view. Their position appears to have been summarized in Article 2(c) of the United Nations Charter of Economic Rights and Duties of States, which provided that each state has the right to expropriate foreign property, that the exercise of this right is not subject to any condition beyond the duty to pay "appropriate" compensation having regard to all the circumstances, that a host country is not required to give foreign companies preferential treatment, and that a state also has the right to revise and renegotiate contracts it has made with foreign companies.[29] The lack of consensus on the international rules applicable to foreign investments created uncertainty in the minds of investors as to the degree of legal protection they might expect under international law. To gain such certainty, the host countries of these investors undertook to conclude a series of bilateral investment treaties that would provide clear rules and effective enforcement mechanisms, at least with regard to their treaty partners. Their primary goal was therefore *protection* of investments made by their nationals and companies. A secondary objective has been to *facilitate* the entry and operation of these investments by inducing host countries, through the treaty, to remove various impediments in their regulatory systems. Developing countries, for their part, signed BITs as a means to *promote* foreign investment and increase the amount of capital and associated technology that would flow to their territories. The basic assumption of this aspect of the BIT is that a bilateral treaty with clear and enforceable rules to protect and facilitate foreign investment reduces risks that the investor would otherwise face and that a reduction in risk, all other things being equal, encourages investment. In the 1980's and 1990's, as capital became less available from other sources such as commercial banks and official aid, developing countries increasingly felt the need to promote foreign investment in order to foster economic development, and they saw BITs as one means of pursuing a campaign of investment promotion. They therefore signed them in increasing numbers, a trend likely to continue until well into the twenty-first century.[30]

---

[28] *See* Restatement (Third) of the Foreign Relations Law of the United States s.712 (1987).

[29] *Report of the Second Committee*, U.N. Doc. A/9946 (1974) and G.A. Res. 3281, 29 UN GAOR Supp. (No.31) at 50, UN Doc. A/9631 (1974).

[30] For a periodically updated collection of bilateral investment treaties from throughout the world, see generally International Center for Settlement of Investment Disputes, *Investment Promotion and Protection Treaties* (1983).

The BIT movement will certainly continue, and the network of treaty relationships is bound to become increasingly more dense in the years ahead. Consequently, counsel to a U.S. investor considering an investment in a particular foreign country should always determine whether a relevant bilateral treaty exists between the United States and the prospective host country. It may also be possible, under certain limited circumstances, for a U.S. enterprise through a wholly or partially owned foreign subsidiary to take advantage of a bilateral investment treaty between the foreign country in which the subsidiary is established and the potential host country in question. As will be seen, many modern treaties contain specific language to prevent such a result. Nonetheless, variations in language among bilateral treaties may make it worthwhile for counsel to explore this possibility in appropriate cases.

It is difficult to determine with any precision whether bilateral commercial treaties in general, or BITs in particular, in fact encourage direct foreign investment and actually influence the foreign investment decisions of American corporations.[31] The existence of bilateral investment treaty with the United States is a signal among other signals that U.S. investment is welcome in the host country. And certainly to the extent that a BIT contains strong guarantees on convertibility of currency and protection from expropriation, it would seem to encourage investment. In discussing the question of the entry of foreign investment, this section will first examine applicable language from the older FCN treaties and will then discuss the newer bilateral investment treaties.

[B] FCN Treaty Provisions on Investments

While many of the early bilateral treaties affecting foreign investment bear the formal designation of "Treaties of Friendship, Commerce and Navigation," some have other titles, including "Agreement of Economic Cooperation," "Treaty of Amity and Economic

---

[31] Salacuse, *BIT By BIT: The Growth of Bilateral Investment Treaties and Their Impact on Foreign Investment in Developing Countries* 24 The Int'l Lawyer 655-675(1990); Comment, *The BIT Won't Bite: The American Bilateral Investment Treaty Program*, 22 Am. U.L. Rev. 931, 942-943 (1984). *Cf.* Malecek, *United States Bilateral Non-Tariff Commercial Treaty Practice: A Section Membership Survey*, 10 Int'l Law. 561 (1976) (an empirical survey of U.S. attorneys concerning their reliance on and uses of bilateral commercial treaties in transnational legal practice).

Relations," and "Treaty of Establishment."[32] Such U.S. treaties are by no means uniform, but each has usually been shaped to meet the needs of the parties concerned through diplomatic negotiations. In specifying the standard of treatment applicable to their respective nationals, the parties to the treaties normally provide that the nationals of each other's country are to receive either "most-favored-nation treatment," that is, that U.S. nationals will not be discriminated against as compared to other aliens and will receive the best treatment accorded to foreigners; or "national treatment," which means that U.S. nationals shall be treated as well as the nationals of the host country.[33] In certain cases the treaty may use another standard, or even a combination of standards. In the post-war era, the U.S. has sought to achieve national treatment for its nationals on the assumption that such treatment is the most advantageous. It should be noted, however, that whether national or most-favored-nation treatment is the more advantageous will depend on the laws in force in the host country and on the other treaties to which it is already a party. Normally, the agreed treatment is to be accorded to both natural persons and legal persons, such as corporations; however, most treaties contain a qualification that U.S. corporations, controlled directly or indirectly by non-U.S. nationals, may not benefit from its provisions.[34]

The treaty usually provides that the nationals and companies of either country are to be accorded national treatment when engaging in all types of commercial, industrial, financial, and other business activity, except for those specifically excluded, within the territories of the other party, whether directly or by agent, or through any form of lawful juridical entity. In order to allow a foreign national to carry out such business activities, the treaty normally permits the nationals and companies of each party within the territory of the other party "(a) to establish and maintain branches, agencies, offices, factories and

---

[32] This section will not consider "Investment Guarantee Agreements" which are normally concluded by exchange of notes between the United States and the host country to allow the Overseas Private Investment Corporation (OPIC) to insure investments in the host country. For a discussion of OPIC, see ch. 28, *Foreign Investment Insurance*.

[33] *See* Walker, *Modern Treaties of Friendship, Commerce and Navigation*, 42 Minnesota Law Review 805, 811 (1950).

[34] Norton, *The Renegotiability of United States Bilateral Commercial Treaties with Member States of the European Economic Community*, 8 Texas International Law Review 299, 310.

other establishments appropriate to the conduct of their business; (b) to organize companies under the general company laws of such other Party . . .; and (c) to control and manage enterprises which they have established or acquired. . . ."[35] In addition, they also often provide: "nationals and companies of either Party shall be accorded within the territories of the other Party: (a) national treatment with respect to leasing land, buildings, and other immovable property appropriate to the conduct of activities in which they are permitted to engage . . . and for residential purposes, and with respect to occupying and using such property; and (b) other rights in immovable property permitted by the applicable laws of the other Party."[36]

At the same time, most bilateral treaties permit the host country to exercise some controls over the entry of investments by foreigners. First, it appears that no bilateral treaty expressly allows the free entry of "capital" into either country concerned;[37] in fact, such agreements or their protocols usually contain specific language permitting capital controls. Thus, for instance, the protocol to the Friendship, Commerce and Navigation Treaty with Japan of 1953 provides that "either Party may impose restrictions on the introduction of foreign capital as may be necessary to protect its monetary reserves. . . ."[38] Secondly, U.S. bilateral treaties often contain language similar to the following: nothing in the treaty shall "prevent either Party from prescribing special formalities in connection with the establishment of alien-controlled enterprises within its territories; but such formalities may not impair the substance of the rights set forth in said paragraph."[39] Such provision allows the host government to enforce certain organizational requirements, for instance, as to residence or nationality of incorporators or directors, so long as the formalities do not materially alter the basic right of entry granted.[40] Third, nearly all bilateral treaties provide mutual reservations allowing the parties to control alien entry into certain fields, such as mining or natural resource

---

[35] *See* Treaty of Friendship, Commerce and Navigation, April 2, 1953, United States-Japan, art. VII, § 1, 4 U.S.T. 2063, 2069, T.I.A.S. No. 2863 [hereinafter cited as U.S.-Japan Treaty of Friendship].

[36] *Id.* art. IX, § 1, at 2071.

[37] A. Fatouros, Government Guarantees to Foreign Investors at (1962).

[38] Protocol, U.S.-Japan Treaty of Friendship *supra* n.35, § 6 at 2082.

[39] U.S.-Japan Treaty of Friendship, *supra* n.35, at art. VII, § 3, at 2070.

[40] A. Fatouros, *supra* n.37, at 143, Walker, *Provisions in United States Commercial Treaties*, 50 Am. J. Int'l L. 373, 387 (1956).

development, banking, insurance, transportation or communications.[41] Although these provisions may exclude entry altogether, more often they allow limited entry, to be directly controlled by the host country.

Finally, the treaty's standard of treatment applicable to entry may affect the amount of control the host country retains. National treatment is usually the most open policy, and provides the least possibility for alien entry controls because aliens are to be treated similarly to nationals. On the other hand, most-favored-nation treatment as to investment entry requires only that the host country treat the entering party no less favorably than the most-favored other aliens entering for business purposes. This means, of course, that rigorous investment controls or screening processes can be employed as long as they are applied without discrimination.[42] So, for instance, the U.S. Treaty of Friendship and Commerce with Pakistan provides that, "each Party reserves the right to limit the extent to which aliens may establish or acquire interests in enterprises engaged within its territories in activities for gain (business activities) provided that in any event not less than most-favored-nation treatment shall be accorded."[43] It should be noted that screening processes may be used indirectly even if a bilateral treaty sets a national treatment standard and appears free of other entry restrictions. In these cases, entry is theoretically free, but government approval may be needed to receive certain tax or other investment incentives, without which entry may not be economically feasible.[44]

In general, it may be said that no bilateral treaty to which the United States is a party guarantees the U.S. investor unconditional freedom of entry without the possibility of restriction. Nonetheless, the existence of a bilateral treaty between the United States and a potential host country may facilitate undertaking the investment and may afford various protections to its continued operation. These agreements, as will be seen, are more significant with respect to the protection of foreign investments and the settlement of investment disputes with the

---

[41] *See, e.g.*, U.S.-Japan Treaty of Friendship, *supra* n.35, art. VII, § 2, at 2069. *See generally* A. Fatouros, *supra* n.37, at 42–43.

[42] The United State Council of the International Chamber of Commerce, *Rights of Businessmen Abroad* 9 (1960); *Foreign Investment, International Law and National Development* 36 (J. Zorn & P. Bayne, eds. 1974).

[43] Treaty of Friendship and Commerce, November 12, 1959, United States - Pakistan, art. VII, § 2, 12 U.S.T. 110, 114, T.I.A.S. No. 4683.

[44] *See, e.g., id.* art. XI, § 5 at 116. *See generally* A. Fatouros, *supra* n.37, at 38.

host country *after* the host country has permitted the entry of a particular investment in question.

[C] Bilateral Investment Treaty Provisions

The principal difference between the early FCN Treaties and the modern bilateral investment treaty is that the later is intended to govern investments exclusively and provides for a more comprehensive treatment of the subject than did the FCN treaties. Although the world's seven hundred BITs (as of 1995) differ in many respects, they all pursue the two basic goals mentioned above of investment promotion and protection. This duality of goals is underscored by the title of most BITs: "Treaty for the Promotion and Protection of Investments," or some variation thereof.

The BITs pursue the objective of protection by establishing international rules about the host country's treatment of foreign investment—rules which restrain the ability of host governments in dealing with foreign investors and investments—and it also provides for an international mechanism, outside the jurisdiction of the host country, to enforce the rules in cases of dispute. The goal of investment promotion is to be achieved by the host country's creation of a stable legal environment that favors foreign investment. The basic working assumption of the BITs is that clear and enforceable rules that protect foreign investors reduce risk, and a reduction in risk promotes investment.

On the other hand, the BITs place no obligation on the home country to take measures to encourage its investors and companies to invest abroad. The obligation of investment promotion is the host country's, not the home country's. Developing countries have sometimes entered into BIT negotiations with the expectation that their industrialized treaty partner would take affirmative action to encourage its nationals to invest in that developing country—an expectation no doubt raised by the word "encouragement" and "promotion" in the treaty. Capital-exporting states, with one or two vaguely stated exceptions, have steadfastly refused to agree to any provision in a BIT obligating them to encourage and induce their nationals to invest in the territories of the BIT partners.[45] A bilateral investment treaty purports to create a symmetrical relationship between the two contracting states, for it provides that the nationals and companies of *either* party to the treaty

---

[45] UNCTC, *Bilateral Investment Treaties* 67 (1988).

may invest under the same conditions and be treated in the same way in the territory of the other. In reality, of course, in a BIT between an industrialized country and a developing nation, an asymmetry exists between the parties since one state (the industrialized country) will be the source and the other state (the developing country) the recipient of virtually all investment flows between the two countries. Thus in theoretically opening its doors through a BIT to investment from a developing country, the industrialized state knows that its own national enterprises are unlikely to face serious competition from enterprises of its treaty partner or that its treaty partner's investments are unlikely to affect the industrialized state's strategic economic interests. It is the threat of such foreign competition and the challenges to its domestic economic interests that are principal concerns of all host countries with respect to inward flows of direct foreign investment.

Although the precise provisions of BITs are not uniform, virtually all BITs treat the same issues. These issues constitute the basic structure of any bilateral investment treaty. The basic structure of any BIT encompasses eight topics:

1. Scope of Application
2. Conditions for the Entry of Foreign Investment
3. General Standards of Treatment of Foreign Investments
4. Monetary Transfers
5. Operational Conditions of the Investment
6. Protection Against Expropriation and Dispossession
7. Compensation for Losses
8. Investment Dispute Settlement

This section will consider the BIT provisions with respect to each of these issues.

[1] Scope of Application

An initial question for counsel in analyzing a BIT is to ascertain the types persons and investments covered by the treaty. The U.S. BITs define both in very broad terms. Key elements in any bilateral investment treaty are its provisions on the BIT's scope of application: the definition of the investors and the investments that may benefit from the agreement. The principles on scope of application are generally found at the beginning of the BIT in articles defining "investors," "companies," "nationals," "investments," and "territory." In a BIT, a contracting state only owes obligations to investors of other contracting states who make investments in the former's territory or areas. It owes no obligations under the BIT to persons or investments which do not come within the definitions of these terms as set out in the treaty document.

In defining the nature of covered investments, the BITs take four basic definitional dimensions into consideration:

a. the form of the investment;

b. the area of the investment's economic activity;

c. the time when the investment is made; and

d. the connection of the investor with the other contracting state.

[a] Form of the Investment

Most BITs define the concept of investment broadly so as to include all sorts of investment forms: tangible and intangible assets, property, and rights. The United States BITS define investment to mean "every kind of investment in the territory of one Party owned or controlled directly or indirectly by nationals or companies of the other Party, such as . . ." and it then proceeds to state a long list of specified types of assets such as tangible and intangible and moveable and immovable property, shares, stocks and bonds of companies, intellectual property and "any right conferred by law or contract or by virtue of any licenses and permits granted pursuant to law."[46] The BIT's goal is to be as inclusive as possible; consequently the specific types of investments mentioned are purely illustrative rather than exclusive. Unlike the FCNs, the new BITs do not make a distinction in their coverage between branches of foreign companies and locally incorporated subsidiaries. Both are covered under the BIT, whereas the U.S. Supreme Court in *Sumitomo Shoji America, Inc. v. Avagliano*[47] had held that the privilege of engaging "accountants and other technical experts, executive personnel, attorneys, agents and other specialists of their choice," granted under the U.S.-Japan Treaty of Friendship,

---

[46] *E.g.*, Art. I, Kazakhstan: Treaty Concerning the Reciprocal Encouragement and Protection of Investment, May 19, 1992, U.S.-Kazakhstan, S. Treaty Doc. No. 11, 103d Cong., 1st Sess. (1993) (entered into force Jan. 12, 1994).

[47] 457 U.S. 176 (1982).

Commerce and Navigation applied only to *branches* of Japanese companies. The Court held that a subsidiary incorporated in the United States was not a company of Japan under the treaty and therefore not covered by the treaty provisions. The BIT's protective provisions, unlike those of the FCN, focus on the investment rather than on the form the enterprise takes.

Thus, in contrast to the FCN treaties which used the term "property," rather than investment, the approach of most modern BITs is to give the term "investment" a broad, non-exclusive definition, recognizing that investment forms are constantly evolving in response to the creativity of investors and the rapidly changing world of international finance.

[b] Economic Area of Activity

Although BITs purport to encourage investments generally by the other party's nationals and companies, in fact they all reserve certain economic sectors for special treatment and limitations. The United States BITs usually contain an annex where such limited or excepted sectors are listed.

[c] Time of Investment

A BIT's coverage of investments also has a time dimension. The specific issue is whether investments made prior to the entry into force of the treaty nonetheless benefit from its provisions. Developing countries have sometimes sought to limit a BIT's application to future investment only or at least to investments made in the relatively recent past. Viewing the BIT as an investment promotion mechanism, they have claimed to see little purpose in granting an incentive for investments already in the host country. Moreover, they argue that their governmental authorities might not have approved such investments had they realized that the investment's rights and privileges would later be expanded by a BIT. Capital-exporting states, on the other hand, have generally sought to protect all investments made by their nationals and companies, regardless of the time when they were made. For example, the U.S. model BIT provides: "[This Treaty] shall apply to investments existing at the time of entry into force as well as to investments made or acquired thereafter."[48]

---

[48] Art. XIII (2), Appendix 27D, *infra*.

BITs also seek to continue to provide protection to an investor once the treaty has terminated or the host country has withdrawn from it. They generally state that investments made under the treaty shall continue to benefit from its provisions for a period of ten years from the effective date of termination.[49] This continuing effects provision is designed to protect investors who have made an investment in reliance on the expectation of treaty protection.

[d] Investor's Connection With Contracting State

Determining which investors can benefit from the treaty is an important issue, since the goal of each contracting state is to secure benefits for its own nationals, companies and investors, not those of third countries. The problem is essentially one of determining what kind of link needs to exist between an investor and a party to a treaty in order to benefit from that treaty's provisions. In the case of physical persons, the task is not difficult since BITs usually rely on nationality or citizenship, a status that can be determined relatively easily under the law of the states involved. Thus the usual provision in U.S. BITs is that a "national" of a Party means a natural person who is a national of a Party under its applicable law.

For investors that are companies or other legal persons, the problem of determining an appropriate link with a contracting state is more complex since such legal forms may be created and owned by persons who have no real connection with any countries that are parties to the treaty. In particular, three types of cases raise problems in this respect:

1) companies organized in a treaty country by nationals of a non-treaty country;

2) companies organized in a non-treaty country by nationals of a treaty country; and

3) companies in which nationals of a non-treaty country have a substantial interest.

For a company to be covered by the treaty, most BITs require that a treaty partner have one or more of the following relations to that company:

---

[49] *E.g.*, Art. XII (4), Turkey: Treaty Concerning the Reciprocal Encouragement and Protection of Investments, Dec. 3, 1985, U.S.-Turk., S. Treaty Doc. No. 19, 99th Cong., 2d Sess. (1986) (entered into force May 18, 1990). Reprinted in 25 Int'l Legal Materials 85 (1986).

1) country of the company's incorporation;
2) country of the company seat, registered office, or principal place of business;
3) country whose nationals have control over or a substantial interest in the company making the investment.

Sometimes these requirements are combined so that an investing company must satisfy two or more to qualify for coverage under the BIT. In order to prevent these provisions from being abused by nationals and companies of non-contracting states, most BITs also provide for certain exceptions. Thus, for example, Article I (2) the United States BIT with Kazakhstan gives each Contracting Party the right to deny the advantages of the Treaty to a company if it is owned or controlled by third country nationals, or in the case of a company of the other Party, that company has no substantial business in the territory of the other Party or is controlled by nationals of a third country with which the denying country does not maintain normal economic relations.

To be protected under a BIT, the Investor must "own" or "control" the Investment. While determining ownership is usually easy, "control" is a more vague and ambiguous concept. In order to give some specificity to the term, control has been dealt with in the text of the BIT itself or in separate protocols or exchange of letters. The concern here has been to prevent persons and companies having no genuine link with treaty partners from obtaining benefits under the treaty.

[2] Conditions of Admission of Foreign Investment

The totality of obligations which a host country owes in its behavior toward a foreign investor is generally referred to in BITs as the "treatment" to be accorded to the investor or the investment. The BITs make a distinction between the treatment to be accorded an investor in making an investment and the treatment to be given after the investment is made.

With respect to the former, virtually all BITs contain a general provision to the effect that "each contracting state shall encourage and create favorable conditions for investors of the other Contracting party to make investments in its territory. . ."[50] Despite the requirement

---

[50] *E.g.*, Art. 3(1), Agreement between the Government of the United Kingdom of Great Britain and Northern Ireland and the Government of the Republic of India, 14 March 1994, for the Promotion and Protection of Investments, *reprinted in* 34 Int'l Legal Materials 935 (1995).

of creating favorable conditions for investment, no BIT requires a host country to admit any investment proposed by an investor from another treaty country. The laws of most countries regulate the entry of foreign capital, and most developing countries in BIT negotiations have taken the position that investments will be admitted in their territories only in accordance with their laws.[51] A common provision in the BITS of many countries is that the host country ". . . shall admit investments in conformity with its laws." This provisions does not appear in most U.S. BITs, however. Nonetheless, a grant of national treatment provided by most US BITs means that a U.S. investor most follow all the laws applicable to a national investment.

In the negotiation of some BITs, capital-exporting states have sought to protect their nationals and companies from unfavorable discrimination by securing treatment on admission that is no less favorable that the treatment given to the making of investments by nationals of the host country or nationals of a third country. For example, Article II (1) of the U.S. BIT Prototype provides:

> Each party shall permit and treat such investments, and activities associated therewith, on a basis no less favorable than that accorded in like situation to investments and associated activities of its own nationals or companies, or of nationals and companies of any third party, whichever is the more favorable.

The implication of this provision is clear: in deciding on admission of a foreign investment project, the host country must treat applications by investors of its treaty partner the same as it treats applications by its own national investors or those from other countries. For countries seeking to encourage investments by its own nationals, such a provision may raise problems. For one thing, the host country may have closed certain sectors to foreign investment for strategic or political reasons. For another, most developing countries give special preference to national investors because they feel that national investors cannot compete on equal footing with foreign firms. They therefore would probably find it easier to grant most-favored nation

---

[51] *E.g.*, The U.K.-Hungary BIT, article 2, provides: "Each Contracting party . . . , subject to its right to exercise powers conferred by its laws, shall admit . . . capital [of the other contracting party." Agreement Between the Government of the United Kingdom of Great Britain and Northern Ireland and the Government of the Hungarian People's Republic for the Promotion and Reciprocal Protection of Investments, March 9, 1987, *reprinted in* 4 ICSID Review - Foreign Investment Law Journal 159 (1989).

treatment on the entry of foreign investment than they would national treatment.

On the other hand, the application of the concepts of national treatment and most-favored-nation treatment to foreign investment projects, no two of which are exactly alike, are far more difficult than they are to international trade in fungible goods, where these concepts were first developed. The qualifying words "in like situations" contained in the clause quoted above may also allow differing treatment with respect to the entry of investments if the projects themselves or the surrounding circumstances are sufficiently dissimilar. Moreover, treaties that have included this type of entry provision also include a specific list of areas and sectors in which foreign investment may be prohibited. For example, the United States-Grenada Treaty grants most-favored-nation and national treatment with respect to the entry of investment from each country, but it also stipulates the following provision:

> . . . subject to the right of each Party to make or maintain exceptions falling within one of the sectors to which the respective host countries may restrict investment by the other country.[52] The list with respect to Grenada consists of the following areas: air transportation; government grants; government insurance and loan programs; ownership of real estate; use of land and natural resources.

Host countries often impose "performance requirements," such as the necessity of using a minimum amount of local content or exporting a minimum amount of product, on a proposed investment project as a condition for admission. As noted above, the United States and certain other capital-exporting states have objected to their use and were successful in securing the adoption of the WTO's Agreement on Trade-Related Investment Measures which would limit them significantly. Since launching its BIT program, the United States has also sought to eliminate their use on a bilateral basis. In distinct contrast to the BIT's advanced by other developed countries, the United States has sought to protect its investors from performance requirements through the BIT process. The U.S. BIT Prototype, article II(4), provides:

---

[52] Art. II, Treaty between the United States of America and Grenada concerning the Reciprocal Encouragement and Protection of Investment, May 2, 1986, (Treaty Doc. 99-25).

Neither Party shall impose performance requirement as a condition of the establishment, expansion, operation, or maintenance of investments, which requires or enforces commitments to export goods produced, or which specify that goods or services must be purchased locally, or which impose any other similar requirements.

Many developing countries have sought to avoid or soften this obligation. Thus the U.S.-Turkey BIT, instead of stipulating an outright prohibition on performance requirements, states that ". . . each Party shall seek to avoid performance requirements as a condition of establishment, expansion or maintenance of investments. . ." (Art. II (7))

The concern with performance requirements, as measures that unjustifiably burden trade and investment, was further developed in the Uruguay Round of the GATT, which produced an Agreement on Trade-Related Investment Measures, forbidding the imposition of measures that are inconsistent with GATT's article III on national treatment and article XI on the elimination of quantitative restrictions. It thus will prevent GATT members from making local content and trade balancing requirements as a condition for the making or operation of foreign investment projects.[53]

[3] General Standards of Treatment For Investments Once Made

BITs stipulate in terms of treaty obligations the standard of treatment which a host country must accord to a foreign investment after it is actually made. They do so in two respects. They define certain general standards of treatment and also state specific standards for certain particular matters, such as monetary transfers, the employment of foreign personnel, and the resolution of disputes with the host government. This section will examine the general treatment standards, while succeeding sections will discuss treatment with regard to specific matters.

One may divide the general standard of treatment, as found in BITs, into seven component parts: a) fair and equitable treatment; b) the provision of constant protection and security; c) protection from unreasonable and discriminatory measures; d) treatment no less than that accorded by international law; and e) a requirement to respect

---

[53] See § 19.06[C][2], supra.

obligations made to investors and investments; f) national treatment; and g) most-favored nation treatment.

[a] Fair and Equitable Treatment

One of the most common standards of treatment found in BITs is an obligation that the host country is to accord foreign investment "fair and equitable treatment."[54] Fair and equitable treatment is a classic formulation of international law and has been the subject of much commentary and state practice.[55] Nonetheless, its precise meaning in a specific question is open to a variety of interpretations.

[b] Full Protection and Security

Another general standard of treatment found in most BITs is the obligation of the host country to accord "full protection and security" to investments made by nationals and companies of its treaty partners. Sometimes BIT's phrase this obligation in terms of "the most constant protection and security." Both terms have been subject to interpretation over the years. Two recent cases interpreting them within the context of bilateral treaties held that the standard does not make the host country responsible for all injuries that befall the investment.[56] Although the host country is thus not a guarantor, it is liable where it has failed to show due diligence in protecting the investor from harm. One definition of due diligence, cited with favor by an ICSID arbitral tribunal, is ". . .reasonable measures of prevention which a well administered government could be expected to exercise under similar circumstances."[57] Consequently, the failure by a host country to take reasonable measures to protect the investment against threats from brigands or violence by police and security officers—common

---

[54] Mohamed I. Khalil, *Treatment of Foreign Investment in Bilateral Investment Treaties,* 7 ICSID Review—Foreign Investment Law Journal 339, 351 (1992).

[55] UNCTC, *Bilateral Investment Treaties* 41-45 (1988).

[56] Compare the ICSID arbitration case of Asian Agricultural Products, Ltd. v. The Republic of Sri Lanka, 27 June 1990, 6 ICSID Review—Foreign Investment Law Journal 526-573 (1991), where the arbitral tribunal interpreted the words "full protection and security" in the U.K.-Sri Lanka bilateral investment treaty, with the I.C.J. decision in Elettronica Sicula S.P.A.(Elsi), 1989 I.C.J. 15, in which the ICJ chamber interpreted the words "constant protection and security" in the 'U.S.-Italy Treaty of Friendship, Commerce and Navigation.

[57] Asian Agricultural Products, Ltd. v. The Republic of Sri Lanka, *supra* n.56, citing Freeman, *Responsibility of States* 15-16 (1957).

events in some countries—might render a Contracting Party liable to compensate an injured investor under a BIT.

[c] Protection Against Arbitrary or Discriminatory Measures

Many BITs provide that ". . . neither Party shall in any way impair by arbitrary or discriminatory measures the management, operation, maintenance, use, enjoyment, acquisition, expansion or disposal of investments." Here, too, is a general standard of treatment that is open to a variety of interpretations.

[d] International Law

Many BITs provide that in no case should investments be given a treatment less favorable than that which is required by international law. This then constitutes the very minimum standard of treatment.

[e] Contractual Obligations

To the extent that a contracting party has entered in obligations with an investor or investment, most BITs require a contracting state to observe those obligations. This provision then acts as counter to the claim that host countries should be able to revise unilaterally contracts which they have made with foreign investors.

[f] National Treatment

Many bilateral treaties, with various exceptions and qualifications,provide that the host country shall; treat investments from its treaty partners in the same way it treats investments by host nationals and companies. All capital-exporting countries attach great importance to this standard, known as national treatment, and their prototype BITs invariably include it. The breadth of this obligation is even greater than one might ordinarily suppose, for the treaty language may require a host country to treat foreign investors on a par with state-owned enterprises, a requirement that may be particularly difficult for socialist countries where the primary domestic investors are usually government corporations. As noted above, many BITS allow a country exceptions from the obligation of national treatment, if such exceptions fall within one of the sectors or matters specified by the Parties in the annex to the treaty. Thus, the U.S. prototype exempts the United States from granting equality of treatment in such economic sectors as air transportation, coastal shipping, banking, insurance, and the ownership and operation of radio and television stations. But even in such excepted areas, the U.S. model treaty requires the Parties to treat one another no less favorably than they treat investment in those areas from third countries.

Some developing countries, recognizing the disparity in financial and technological resources between their own national enterprises and those of multinational corporations have sought to limit the scope of this national treatment obligation. At the very least, they have created exceptions, as, for example, when a host country has reserved certain economic sectors for development by its own public enterprise and private entrepreneurs.

[g] Most-Favored-Nation Treatment

Many BITs contain "most-favored-nation clauses" that guarantee treaty-protected investments will receive treatment at least as favorable as the treatment the host country grants to investments by nationals and companies from any third state. A typical formulation is found in the Netherlands-Philippines BIT: "Each Contracting Party shall extend to investments in its territory treatment no less favorable than that granted to investments of any third state."[58]

[h] Both National Treatment and Most-Favored-Nation Treatment

Many BITs combine both national treatment and most-favored-nation treatment so that the foreign investor may take advantage of whichever standard of treatment is the more favorable. Capital-exporting desire to secured this combined standard because it assures them equality of treatment with both host country nationals and companies and with investors from third countries.

[4] Monetary Transfers

For any foreign investment project, the ability to repatriate income and capital, to pay foreign obligations in another currency, and to purchase raw materials and spare parts from abroad is crucial to the project's success. For this reason, capital-exporting states in BIT negotiations have pressed for unrestricted freedom for investors to make these monetary operations, which are collectively referred to as

---

[58] Agreement for the Promotion and Protection of Investment, Feb. 27, 1985, Netherlands-Philippines, Art. 3, 1985 Trachtatenblad (Neth.) No. 86.

"transfers."[59] On the other hand, chronic balance of payments difficulties of many host countries and their need to conserve foreign exchange to pay for essential goods and services considerably reduce their ability and their willingness to grant foreign investors the unrestricted right to make monetary transfers. For this reason, most developing countries have exchange-control laws to regulate the conversion and transfers of currency abroad. As a result of this fundamental conflict in goals, the negotiation of BIT provisions on monetary transfers has often been among the most difficult to conclude. Capital-exporting countries seek broad, unrestricted guarantees on monetary transfers while developing countries press for limited guarantees subject to a variety of exceptions.

The monetary transfer provisions of most BITs deal with five basic issues:

1) the general nature of the investor's rights to make monetary transfers;

2) the type of payments that are covered by the right to make transfers;

3) the nature of the currency with which the payment may be made;

4) the applicable exchange rate; and

5) the time within which the host country must allow the investor to make transfers.

The U.S. BIT approach to monetary transfers is represented by Article IV, paragraph 1, of the Turkey-United States Bilateral Investment Treaty, which states the basic rule: "Each party shall permit all transfers related to an investment to be made freely and without delay into and out of its territory." U.S. BITs then proceed to state a non-exclusive list of what may be transferred freely, including returns, payments under contracts, proceeds from the sale or liquidation of any part of an investment, payments arising out of the settlement of any dispute, and additional contributions to capital for the maintenance or development of an investment. Moreover, in view of the structure of this BIT provision, it can be argued that other types of payments, not specifically mentioned are permitted if they fit within the general concept of "transfer" with respect to an investment. For example,

---

[59] Mohamed I. Khalil, *Treatment of Foreign Investment in Bilateral Investment Treaties,* 7 ICSID Review—Foreign Investment Law Journal 339, 360 (1992).

payments for the purchase of spare parts would presumably be covered, although not specifically mentioned, because, being made according to a sales agreement, they constitute "payments under a contract." "Return" is also a broad concept which means "an amount derived from or associated with an investment including profits, dividends, interest, capital gain, royalty payment, management, technical assistance or other fee or returns in kind."

BITs provide that transfers are to be made without delay and in a freely convertible currency. With respect to currency rates of exchange, most U.S. BITs state that "transfers shall be made at the market rate of exchange existing on the date of the transfer with respect to spot transactions in the currency to be transferred."

BITs sometimes place limitations on the right of an investment to make monetary transfers due to a host country's need to protect its balance of payments. In addition, a host country may limit monetary transfers in order to protect the rights of creditors or ensure compliance with securities laws or with laws on the satisfaction of judgments, provided such measures are "equitable, non-discriminatory, and a good faith application of its laws and regulations." For example, this provision might allow a central bank, before authorizing a transfer, to require a showing by the investor that it is not subject to an unsatisfied judgment or attachment in connection with a debt it owes. Such a requirement, of course, could serve to delay the transfer and thus avoid one of the essential elements of the freedom of transfer—that it be made without delay.

[5] Operational Conditions

BITs sometimes provide treatment standards with respect to certain operational conditions, such as the investor's right to enter the country, employ foreign nationals and be free of performance requirements. One of the most important, of course, is for the investor's employees to be able to enter the host country and to manage and operate the investment. Most BITs do not grant the investor an automatic right to enter and stay in the host country. German BITs provide that each contracting party will give "sympathetic consideration" to applications for entry, and United States BITs give "nationals" of contracting parties the right to enter the other contracting state for purposes of establishing or operating investments subject to the laws of the host country. In this connection, one might refer to the United States

Supreme Court case of Sumitomo Shoji America, Inc. v. Avagliano,[60] in which the Court had to interpret the provisions of the U.S.-Japan Treaty of Friendship, Commerce and Navigation giving companies of either Party in the territory of the other the right to engage executive personnel and technical experts "of their choice". In this case, a wholly-owned U.S. subsidiary of a Japanese company was being sued by a group of its female employees under the U.S. civil rights legislation for discriminating against them by hiring only Japanese males to fill executive positions. The Court held against the Japanese subsidiary on the grounds that it was an American company, not a company of "the other Party" (i.e. Japan), since it had been incorporated in the United States.

[6] Compensation for Losses from Armed Conflict or Internal Disorder

Most BITs also deal with losses to an investment due to armed conflict or internal disorder; however, they do not normally establish an absolute right to compensation. Instead, many promise that foreign investors will be treated in the same way as are nationals of the host country with respect to compensation. Thus, if the host country compensates or assists its own nationals whose property has been damaged, it would be required to give similar assistance to foreign investors covered by the bilateral investment treaty. Some treaties may also provide for most-favored-nation treatment on this question. The ICSID case of *Asian Agricultural Products, Ltd. v. The Republic of Sri Lanka*[61] is one of the few cases which has considered this provision in detail in connection with a dispute between an injured investor and a host country government. Among other things, the tribunal, in applying a BIT between Sri Lanka and the United Kingdom, concluded that in addition to any specific compensatory actions taken for the benefit of other investors, this provision would also make applicable to an injured investor any *promised* higher standard, for example in another bilateral investment treaty, granted to investors from other countries.

[7] Protection Against Dispossession

One of the primary functions of any bilateral investment treaty is to protect foreign investments against nationalization, expropriation

---

[60] 457 U.S. 176 (1982).
[61] 27 June 1990, 30 Int'l Legal Materials 580 (1991).

or other forms of interference with property rights by host country governmental authorities. Despite positions taken by third world nations in various multilateral fora, virtually all BITs with developing countries adopt some variation of the traditional western view of international law that a state may not expropriate property of an alien except 1) for a public purpose, 2) in a non-discriminatory manner, 3) upon payment of compensation, and, in most instances, 4) with provision for some form of judicial review. The various elements of the traditional rule have taken different formulations in different treaties, some more and some less protective of investor interests.

It is with respect to the standard of compensation where one notices the greatest variation and where negotiations have been the most difficult. Nonetheless many, if not most, BITs have adopted the substance, if not the form, of the traditional rule, expressed in the so-called "Hull formula" that such compensation must be "prompt, adequate and effective."[62] They then proceed to define the meaning of each of these words.

For example, the Turkey-United States BIT, article III, provides that compensation in cases of expropriation ". . .shall be equivalent to the fair market value of the investment at the time the expropriatory action was taken or became known." The effect of this provision is to make clear that book value, often argued for by host countries in expropriation cases, is not the applicable standard of compensation. BITs also often specify that compensation in cases of expropriation is to include interest at a commercial rate from the date of such expropriation until the payment date and that at the request of the investor it shall be calculated in a freely convertible currency.

[8] Investment Dispute Settlement

For foreign investors and their governments, one of the great deficiencies of customary international law has been its lack of effective and binding mechanism for the resolution of investment disputes. One aim of the BIT movement has been to remedy this situation.

Most recent BITs provide for two distinct dispute settlement mechanisms: one for disputes between the two contracting states and the other for disputes between a host country and an aggrieved foreign

---

[62] Mohamed I. Khalil, *Treatment of Foreign Investment in Bilateral Investment Treaties,* 7 ICSID Review—Foreign Investment Law Journal 339, 360 (1992).

investor. With respect to the former, most BITs provide that in the event of disputes over the interpretation or application of the treaty, the two states concerned will first seek to resolve their differences through negotiation and then, if that fails, through *ad hoc* arbitration.

The trend among more recent BITs is also to provide a separate procedure, normally under the auspices of the International Centre for Settlement of Investment Disputes (ICSID),[63] for the settlement of disputes between an aggrieved foreign investor and the host country government. By concluding a BIT, the two states, in most cases, give the required consent needed to establish ICSID jurisdiction in the event of a future dispute. Although the investor must first try to resolve the conflict through negotiation, it ultimately has the power to invoke compulsory arbitration to secure a binding award.

---

[63] Convention on the Settlement of Investment Disputes Between States and Nationals of Other States, *done* at Washington, March 18, 1965, [1965] 575 U.N.T.S. 159. For a discussion of ICSID, see § 30.03[D], *infra*.

§ 19.07 Host Country Investment Laws and Regulations

[A] In General

As indicated in section 19.06, the ability of a U.S. business to undertake an investment project in a foreign country is subject to the sovereignty of the host country whose laws, regulations, and policies will determine whether and how the investment may be made. National laws and policies toward foreign investment demonstrate extreme diversity throughout the world. On the one hand, some countries–particularly those with a strong socialist orientation requiring all means of production to be in the hands of the state–are virtually closed to equity investment by United States or other foreign enterprises. On the other hand, other countries, which have an exceptional need for capital and technology, have structured their legislation and policies in such a way as to encourage the entry of foreign investment and to provide it with special incentives not normally available to local investors. Moreover, such policies and laws may change significantly over time. For example, the end of Communist rule in Eastern and Central Europe in 1989 and the outbreak of the debt crisis of 1982 have led countries that had severely restricted or even curtailed foreign investment to adopt policies and laws that would actively promote it.

Within individual countries, the foreign investor may encounter numerous laws having an impact on the desirability of undertaking a foreign investment project, including tax laws, antitrust laws, securities and corporate laws, and labor laws, all of which may either expressly or implicitly offer advantages or disadvantages to the contemplated investment project. In addition to constitutional provisions on the right of private property and the power of the state to confiscate wealth, the potential investor must also closely examine the country's general political stability, the honesty and effectiveness of its government, its relevant national policies, both written and unwritten, and the attitudes of government officials toward foreign investment in general and the project in question in particular.

Numerous countries–particularly those in the developing world–have enacted special legislation to govern the entry and operation of foreign investment within their territories. These laws, variously known as "investment laws," "investment promotion statutes," "joint venture laws" or "foreign investment codes," now seem to be a basic element in the legal systems of almost every developing country in the world. Indeed, they are so numerous that the International Centre for Settlement of Investment Disputes (ICSID), an affiliate of the World Bank, has compiled them into a ten volume, loose-leaf series entitled *Investment Laws of the World*,[1] a publication that affords the U.S. lawyer the most comprehensive bibliographic coverage of this type of legislation among developing nations. While such legislation is less common in industrialized countries, it may also be found in Canada, Australia, and Japan. Moreover, even when a country does not have a specific law covering "foreign investment," its legislation regulating foreign exchange, restrictive business practices, and acquisitions may serve to regulate foreign investment activity in its territory.[2]

In addition to a general foreign investment law–or sometimes instead of it–a few countries have separate investment laws for particular economic sectors such as petroleum, agriculture, tourism, or other areas to which the host government particularly wishes to attract foreign capital. Because of the exceptional diversity of the world's foreign investment laws, one can do no more than summarize their general principles in the limited space available in the present chapter. In addition to the ICSID collection of investment laws, an attorney may find detailed treatment on individual countries in a variety of books, articles, and government publications, some of which are listed in the bibliography to this chapter.

Basically, host country foreign investment legislation has two general purposes: to *control* and to *encourage* foreign investment within its territory. In countries actively seeking foreign investment because of a shortage of local capital and technology, the investment codes or laws tend to emphasize the promotion or encouragement function. But, in countries which are skeptical of the benefits of foreign investment by reason of ideology or historical experience–for example, some of those in Latin America–the law has tended to emphasize control rather than promotion.[3] In all legislation, however, one can usually find provisions designed both to encourage and to control the entry and operation of foreign investment. Although with the increased

---

[1] International Centre for Settlement of Investment Disputes (ICSID), *Investment Laws of the World: The Developing Nations* (1977; periodic supplements) [hereinafter cited as *Investment Laws of the World*].

[2] K. Grewlich, Direct Investment in the OECD Countries 49 (1978).

[3] *See generally* United Nations Centre on Transnational Corporations: National Legislation and Regulations (1978).

emphasis throughout the world on market economics and open economies which has developed since the late 1980s, virtually all investment laws have de-emphasized control and greatly increased stress on foreign investment promotion.

The investment law normally constitutes the basic legal framework within the host country for undertaking and operating a foreign investment project. It is not, however, the exclusive applicable legislation, for the project will also have to deal with and be subject to a host of other laws, rules and regulations as well.

The investment law of a country is normally the most authoritative, complete, and detailed statement of government policy toward foreign investment. Indeed, it is often the *only* statement of policy readily available to the investor, as well as to government officials with whom the investor must deal. At the same time, a country's investment law may appear quite general—even vague to the investor. In most cases, the host country government will promulgate regulations or other subordinate legislation to complete the general investment law. It may also provide other information of varying degrees of helpfulness in a wide variety of forms, booklets, and brochures.

Section 19.03 discussed the benefits and costs to the host country of obtaining foreign investment. One of the fundamental purposes of the investment code and related legislation is to create a legal framework that will maximize those potential benefits and minimize the potential costs to the host country. To put the matter in another way, the investment code structures the bargain between the host country and the foreign investor with respect to sharing benefits and costs of foreign investment projects.

In setting down the legal framework for foreign investment in the host country, foreign investment laws and codes, almost without exception, seek to treat four major issues:

(1) the types of investment projects permitted;

(2) the incentives offered to desired foreign investment;

(3) the controls applicable to foreign investment; and

(4) the system for administering the foreign investment law.

The remainder of this section will treat each of these issues in turn.

[B] Defining Permitted Investments

The investment code or other relevant law of the host country will ordinarily seek to define the kind of investment projects which foreigners will be permitted or encouraged to undertake. Despite proclaimed "open-door policies," probably no country, including the United States,[4] will allow foreign nationals to invest in any and all types of economic activity.[5] At the very minimum, considerations of national security and defense will dictate that particularly sensitive industries—such as armaments or telecommunications—be firmly controlled by nationals of the host country, if not by the state itself. Such prohibition may extend far beyond the defense industries, especially when the government wants to prevent foreign domination of important sectors of the economy.

In order to provide guidance to potential investors, the investment legislation of many countries will affirmatively specify those areas of economic activity in which foreign capital will be permitted to operate. Often, the law will define such permitted areas in rather general term similar to the following: "foreign capital shall be permitted to invest in industrialization, mining, energy, tourism, transportation, and other fields." Sometimes the host country will enact separate investment laws for each economic sector to which it is trying to attract foreign capital; consequently, its applicable legislation might consist of an agricultural investment law, an industrial investment law, and a tourism investment law.

Since such general legislative provisions are of limited usefulness in guiding the investor, many developing countries formulate, either

---

[4] U.S. legislation specifically restricts aliens from controlling businesses engaged in banking, insurance, resources and power, air commerce, and certain communications and maritime enterprises. *See A Guide to Foreign Investment Under United States Law* 157 (Committee to Study Foreign Investment in the United States of the Section of Corporation, Banking and Business Law of the American Bar Association, A. Roth, Project Coordinator, 1979); Vila, *Legal Aspects of Foreign Direct Investments in the United States*, 16 Int'l Law. 1 (1982). *See also* for extended discussions of the specific restrictions affecting alien investment in these sectors, *id.* at 157–229; *Foreign Investment in the United States 1980* 311-535 (J. Marans, P. Williams & J. Griffin, eds. 1980). Some U.S. states limit foreign investment in agriculture, often by means of land ownership restrictions. *See State by State Survey of Limitations on Foreign Investment*, in Foreign Investment in the United States 1980, *supra*, at 599–795; Vila, *supra*, at 13–15.

[5] R. Robinson, *Foreign Investment in the Third World: A Comparative Study of Selected Developing Country Investment Promotion Programs* 14 (1980).

by regulation or other administrative act, a list of specific permitted activities that may be undertaken within given economic sectors. In addition, they may prepare actual project proposals to be undertaken by foreign capital. Consequently, the investment law itself represents only a very general framework within which particular project activities are to be defined. The investor must therefore obtain further details and guidance from other regulations and governmental directives.

The definition of a permitted investment will ordinarily include other factors as well as the economic sector in which the project is to operate. In analyzing foreign investment laws and policies, an American attorney should realize that the host country government is not only interested in the nature of the investment as such, but is also concerned with the *contribution* which the investment project will make to the local economy and to the society. That contribution may be measured in a variety of ways, including the number of jobs created, the additional export earnings to be gained, the foreign exchange to be saved, the effect on hard currency reserves, the development of managerial skills, and the real and effective transfer of useable technology to the country.

The law may therefore define permitted investments in such a way as to allow only those kinds of projects which have real potential for making the desired contributions to the economy. For example, on the assumption that joint ventures contribute to the acquisition of managerial skills and technology, some investment laws, in addition to enumerating permitted fields of activities, specify those areas where a foreign investor may operate only in conjunction with local capital. This joint venture requirement faces the investor with a decision as to whether or not to include a partner in its proposed project and, if so, how and where to find an appropriate partner. Joint ventures, an increasingly common vehicles for investment, are treated in greater detail in §§ 19.09 and 19.10, *supra*.

In addition to the fields of permitted investment activity, the investment law may specify the kinds of capital and other resources that may be invested. In order to ensure a net in-flow of new resources to the host country, the law may require that any invested capital emanate from a foreign source; in addition, it may limit the ability of the foreign investor to mobilize and use local capital and resources. The definition of permitted investments may also extend to the type of technology that the project is allowed to use. For example, the 1974

Egyptian law provided that approved projects may only incorporate machinery and equipment "compatible with modern technological developments and [that] have not been previously used. . . ."[6]

Such a provision could of course prevent a multi-national corporation from transferring to a developing country the machinery and equipment already being used by one of its subsidiaries in an industrialized country, a commonly used strategy to extend the life of equipment that has become outmoded. Other provisions affecting the nature of the project may require the project to be located in particular parts of the country–often in those areas which the government particularly wants to develop economically–or may even specify the kind of products the project is to produce.

Often host country governments, in order to earn needed foreign exchange, want foreign investment projects to produce only for export, and they therefore incorporate provisions in the law making it difficult or virtually impossible a project to sell in the local market. The issue of whether permitted investment projects must be "export-oriented" or may instead serve the local market ("import substitution")[7] has often provoked controversy between investors and officials of host country governments. Since investors ordinarily would prefer to serve the local market, this issue has constituted a major obstacle to undertaking investment projects on numerous occasions.

Finally, either the law or policy of the host country may require that permitted projects be a minimum size or that the foreign investor invest a minimum amount of capital. Such requirements are probably based on the assumption that certain projects may be so small as to offer no real benefit to the host country. Conversely, the attorney for the investor should also remember that if a project is sufficiently large, the host country government may be willing to grant special privileges or concessions not ordinarily available to other investments entering the country.

---

[6] Law No. 43 of 1974, as amended by Law No. 32 of 1977. I *Investment Laws of the World* (Arab Republic of Egypt, Text of Law) art. 2, §§ ii, at 4. See Salacuse, *Egypt's New Law on Foreign Investment: The Framework for Economic Openness*, 9 Int'l Law. 647, 650-51 (1975). The Egyptian law allowed the foreign investor to obtain an exemption from the requirement of new machinery and equipment.

[7] "Import substitution" results when companies within the host country produce items for local consumption that were previously imported, thus saving the host country foreign exchange that was formerly needed to pay for the imports.

[C] Investment Incentives

In an effort to attract foreign capital to their territories, the governments of many countries offer special incentives and guarantees to foreign investors. The nature of these incentives and guarantees varies from country to country, and as a group they demonstrate exceptional diversity. They include tax exemptions, direct subsidies, government agreements to purchase a share of production, government guarantees of the project's debts, customs duties exemptions, and priority in the use of government facilities such as railroads and ports. In recent years, debt-to-equity conversion programs and privatization programs, discussed respectively in sections 19.13 and 19.14, *infra*, have been added to these traditional types of incentives.

Underlying this approach to investment promotion is the assumption that investors do not find the host country sufficiently attractive for a direct investment because the prevailing conditions either prevent them from earning adequate returns or confront them with unacceptable risks. The basic thrust of host country incentives and guarantees is therefore either to raise the rate of return which the investor would otherwise earn if it undertook the project, or reduce the risk to which it would be otherwise subjected. Accordingly, one can categorize incentives and guarantees into two categories: 1) those which seek to increase the rate of return, such as tax exemptions, subsidies, and agreements to purchase products at a minimum price; and 2) those which reduce the risk, such as guarantees to provide foreign exchange for debt servicing, agreements for the settlement of any eventual disputes by an international forum, and guarantees against nationalization or expropriation except upon prompt, adequate and effective compensation. One of the biggest risks for the investor, of course, stems from competition by other enterprises. Accordingly, many host countries, in appropriate cases, are prepared to grant the foreign investor a virtual monopoly over the local market by agreeing either 1) to prohibit other similar investments for a specific period of time, and/or, 2) to prevent the importation of competing goods by either a high tariff or an import quota.

Nearly all host countries manipulate their tax and fiscal systems in order to attract foreign investment. One of the most common incentives is the "tax holiday", which exempts the enterprise–and sometimes the investor–from local income and other taxation for a specified period of years. The host country may also grant exemptions from taxes on dividends, royalty payments, interest payments, property taxes, and numerous other charges and fees for which the project, its investors, creditors and contractors would otherwise be liable.[8] Yet another important tax benefit is the grant of a tax exemption to the project's foreign employees. A variation on the tax holiday is "tax stabilization", which guarantees that the approved enterprise will pay no more than a specified maximum tax rate for a determined period of time. An approved project may often obtain the privilege to import capital goods, spare parts, and sometimes raw materials at reduced tariff rates or without the payment of any customs duty whatsoever. Due to the high customs duties prevailing in most developing countries, such customs exemptions may be extremely important to the profitability of the project. Some countries have created "free zones" or "industrial export zones" where export-oriented projects are located and may operate without the payment of export or import duties, on the condition that they do not serve the local market.

In negotiating and drafting an investment agreement that provides such tax and fiscal incentives, counsel for the investor should take great care in understanding the host country's tax system, in determining how its tax laws are applied in practice, and in formulating precisely the nature and extent of any exemption granted. For example, once the project has been undertaken, host country authorities may hold that a provision exempting the project's imports from all "customs duties" will not exempt it from the payment of a "development tax" imposed on imports by a special law.

In many countries, particularly those with a socialist orientation, both public and private enterprises are required to operate within a restrictive set of rules and regulations governing financial management, labor, prices, and numerous other matters. In an effort to attract foreign investment, some governments have been willing to exempt foreign investors from many of these rules and regulations.[9] The exemption from various taxes and laws is one of the most prevalent

---

[8] For a survey of tax incentives in developing countries, see Int'l Bar Association Tax Committee, Section on Business Law, *Tax Incentives for Private Investments in Developing Countries* 181–272 (R. Antoine ed. 1979).

[9] For discussion of this issue with respect to Egypt, see Salacuse, *Foreign Investment and Legislative Exemptions in Egypt: Needed Stimulus or New Capitulations?* in Michalak & Salacuse (eds.), Social Legislation in the Contemporary Middle East 241-261 (1986).

forms of incentive, particularly in developing countries, where governments seem to find them attractive primarily because they do not cost anything, at least in the short run. Yet, incentives may introduce distortions into the economy and create within the host country a group of privileged enterprises that are able to use these exemptions effectively to compete with, and perhaps injure, local business activity.

The investment laws of some countries may grant incentives in proportion to the size of the project, its importance to the economy, or its geographic location in an underdeveloped area. Thus a project of $5 million might obtain a tax holiday of five years, while one of $20 million might receive an exemption of ten years. But regardless of what the law may say with respect to incentives, in some countries it is always possible, because of the size or importance of the project, to negotiate a special agreement with the government to obtain additional incentives and privileges beyond those specified in the law. As a result, the investor with a particularly important project may be able, through negotiation of a special investment agreement or concession agreement, to obtain a wide range of incentives and privileges not specifically granted in the law.

[D] Investment Controls

The investment code will also seek to impose certain controls on the investment project and on the investor itself. Here, again, the nature of those controls varies from country to country and usually reflects the peculiarities of the host country economy, its development objectives, and the government's social and political policies.

The attorney for the foreign investor should be aware of the nature and implications of such controls and attempt to plan the enterprise–as well as its relations with the host country government–in such a way as to mitigate their harshness.

In developing countries where foreign exchange is often in short supply, controls on the acquisition and use of foreign exchange by the investment project often constitute one of the most powerful means of regulating and influencing its activities. Thus, limitations on the availability of foreign exchange for foreign debt servicing, repatriation of profits, and acquisition of spare parts and raw materials can significantly affect, and indeed ultimately curtail, the operations of the project itself. Normally, the rules on these matters are set down in the host country's foreign exchange laws and regulations;[10] however,

---

[10] *See* § 2.04[B], *supra.*

the investment law will ordinarily include special provisions for foreign investment projects. In addition, the appropriate governmental ministry or the Central Bank may enter into a separate agreement or issue a license specifying the particular privileges and controls applicable to the project in question.

Another area of control concerns the nationality of the managers and other employees of the project. In view of the host country's general objective of obtaining new skills and technology and of creating employment for its nationals, it will normally wish to maximize the employment of host country nationals, and it may therefore require, by quota or other means, that the project shape its employment policies accordingly. In order to facilitate this goal, the government may also require the project to develop a training plan for the development of local personnel so that over time indigenous employees may come to occupy virtually all positions in the project. A further type of related control is to be found in the so-called joint venture requirement which permits the investor to undertake a project only in association with local public or private capital.

In many countries, government price controls constitute a major constraint on the operations of an investment project that is selling its products in the local market. Generally, where the government has granted the project a virtual monopoly by establishing high tariffs or quotas on competing goods, it will feel obliged to impose some form of price controls to prevent the project from abusing its monopoly position. Ordinarily, the price is fixed by an order of a government ministry. Over time, as costs of labor, materials, and overhead rise, the project may have to seek periodically an increase in the maximum selling price in order to maintain the profitability of its operations; consequently, the U.S. investor and his counsel may find themselves in a process of virtually constant negotiation with relevant ministry officials over this issue.

Even when the project is formally exempt from price controls, such controls may nevertheless affect operations if they apply to a competitor. It sometimes happens that the competitor is a public sector enterprise and is required to sell its products at a low price, the effect of which is to erode the competitive position of the foreign investment project and prevent it from selling its own products at a profitable price. In such cases, the foreign investor may find itself in the paradoxical position of supporting a competitor's request to the government to raise the applicable price controls on the competitor's products.

The host country may also chose to impose on the project a variety of financing restrictions, including minimum equity requirements, prescribed debt-equity ratios, limitations on the reinvestment of profits, and prohibitions on financing from local sources. It will also be recalled, from Chapter 12 *supra*, that many developing countries also impose restrictions on payments for technology, royalties for trademarks, and technical services.

When the project will operate in a centrally-planned or government-controlled economy, the host country government may impose controls that limit the project's rate of return. As indicated above, if the project will have a virtual monopoly in the local market, the host country government may see fit to impose price controls so that the project does not abuse its quasi-monopolistic position in the country. Transfer pricing–that is, prices charged between affiliates for commodities or services–may be another subject of regulation of the host country.[11] In view of the fact that such dealings cannot be considered arms-length transactions, since the parent may manipulate the price to its subsidiary so as to avoid taxation, the host country government may consider it important to regulate, or at least monitor, such prices. Accordingly, it may institute a system of examination to make sure that the prices represent fair value on the world market. In cases where the foreign investment project is selling commodities to the parent, the host country government may require that such sales be done at its own government "posted price", and it may not accept a figure agreed upon by the two parties concerned.

The controls imposed on a foreign investment project may touch virtually every facet of its operation, and may include restrictions on expansion and reinvestment, as well as the requirement of "disinvestment," that is, the sale of participation in the project to local investors or to the government, over a specified period of time. Investment laws often specify various sanctions for failure to respect the controls imposed on the project, including loss of incentives and privileges, and fines and revocation of the approval to operate. In many cases, however, the law is silent as to such consequences.

The host country government ordinarily imposes these restrictions on the investment project in order to minimize the costs and maximize

---

[11] *See generally* OECD, *Transfer Pricing and Multinational Enterprises* (1979).

the rewards from foreign investment. In practice, however, because of misconceived controls, bureaucratic inertia, corruption, or distortions in the economy, such restrictions sometimes fail to achieve their objective; they often simply increase the difficulties of undertaking and operating the project, while failing to create the benefits desired by the host country. Through a process of negotiation and proper planning, counsel may be able to alleviate some of the harsher results of these controls for the investor.

Since the late 1980s, many countries have eased these controls has they have shifted from command to market economies and as they have recognized a growing need to attract foreign investment to their territories. Consequently, foreign exchange controls have eased or been eliminated in many parts of the world, and most countries instead of insisting on divestment of by foreign investment have themselves been divesting their government of state-owned enterprise through privatization programs to investors from abroad.[12]

[E] Administration of Host Country Investment Laws and Regulations

Any system of host country regulation of foreign investment requires a governmental agency to administer its provisions. Such agencies do indeed exist in most countries of the world, and the lawyer representing a foreign investor spends much time with them in working out the arrangements for undertaking the investment project. It therefore behooves the attorney, before embarking on formal dealings, to understand thoroughly the nature of the body with which he will be working, as well as its procedure and techniques.

The primary reason for the agency's importance resides in the fact that virtually all systems of host country regulation require that the proposed investment project be screened and approved by the agency *before* the investment is undertaken. In the few countries where a direct investment may be made without such screening, the investment law normally provides that prior screening will be required if the project is to receive incentives, such as tax exemptions and other privileges; consequently, for all practical purposes, the investor in such countries will seek approval of the investment before actually undertaking it.

The specific body charged with administering the investment law varies from country to country. In many parts of the world, such body

---

[12] *See* § 19.14, *infra*.

is often separate from the regular government ministries and takes the form of an interministerial committee or an independent agency with representatives from various interested ministries. Some countries give this power to their ministry of planning, and a few of the more developed nations authorize specific ministries to screen investments within their particular sectors of activity. Thus, the ministry of tourism might have the exclusive right to screen a hotel or other touristic project, while the ministry of industry might approve proposals for new factories.

In dealing with such agencies, the U.S. attorney will invariably obtain the assistance of local counsel or specialized consultants. An initial step in the process of investment approval is to determine the precise extent of the agency's real authority and power, and then to become familiar with its procedures. While special interministerial agencies may hold themselves out as "super ministries" capable of providing "one-stop shopping" and of issuing all necessary approvals, in practice the investor may find that even though it has secured approval from the investment agency, it must nonetheless obtain additional permits and licenses from other governmental ministries. For example, even though the investment agency has approved a project calling for the construction of a factory, it may still be necessary to obtain the requisite building permits from the relevant unit of local government before beginning construction. Moreover, technology transfer agreements and loans may be subjected to an additional screening and approval procedure by the Central Bank or Ministry of Finance.

During the approval process, the attorney may also encounter obstructive conflicts and jealousies between the investment organization on the one hand and the functional ministries on the other, or among several competing ministries–factors which may hinder undertaking the project. For example, in one country which had a separate law for investment in industry, administered by the Ministry of Industry, and another law for investment in agriculture, administered by the Ministry of Agriculture, foreign investors proposing to undertake integrated agro-industrial projects found themselves caught squarely in the middle of an intense jurisdictional rivalry between the two ministries. Situations such as these require exceptional diplomatic skills on the part of the foreign investor and its counsel.

Normally, the investment agency or the relevant ministry will have developed special procedures and forms which the investor must complete in order to obtain approval; the assistance of local counsel, whose knowledge of the law, its past application, the practice and policies of the investment agency, and the attitudes of its personnel, will be indispensable in completing the lengthy screening procedure and in obtaining approval. The investor should be aware that completion of these procedures may entail significant expense. For example, many investment agencies will require the submission of a feasibility study, or at least a pre-feasibility study, either of which may be costly. A further element of expense is often caused by the long delays between the time the application is submitted and the time the approval is granted, a period during which the attorney and the executives of the investor will devote considerable time to negotiations with host country officials. While some countries may give such approvals in a very expeditious fashion, others may take a long time, either because of lack of sufficient staff or because of political reasons. Often, when inexperienced personnel staff the investment agency, the investor and his lawyers may have to devote time and effort to educate them.

The lawyer will also have to determine the latitude that the investment agency or ministry has to negotiate the various incentives and restrictions discussed above. Normally, the investment law constitutes a basic framework which grants authority, in varying degrees, to the investment organization to negotiate the particular terms to be accorded the individual foreign investor on such matters as foreign exchange allocation, tax holidays, customs duties exemptions, and other essential matters relating to the establishment and operation of the project. In most instances, obtaining approval for an investment is not automatic, but rather is a matter of negotiation, a process of give and take. Thus, to obtain desirable incentives the investor may have to alter the project to obtain approval from the agency.

Often, in addition to screening project proposals, the investment organization or ministry is supposed to promote and encourage foreign investment in the host country. It may execute this mandate in numerous ways, with varying degrees of effectiveness. Some do virtually nothing, viewing their primary function, regardless of the language of the law, as one of controlling foreign capital. Others provide information on investment opportunities, assist potential investors in finding local partners, and in general play an active role in bringing a proposed investment project to fruition. Still others may develop specific project ideas and actively seek out investors to undertake them.

Once the project has been approved, the agency may have a continuing role in monitoring its development and, once it begins operation, making sure that it meets the obligations and conditions specified in the investment approval or other document. Host country governments are by no means uniformly effective in monitoring investments. Due to problems of inadequate manpower, insufficient resources, and inexact accounting standards, to name just a few, some countries merely give lip service to this concept; however, a few do effectively supervise projects once they have been approved to make sure that all of the conditions and restrictions are respected.

§ 19.08 Host Country Investment Approvals, Licenses, and Agreements

Having decided to approve a particular investment proposal, the relevant host country agency will then authorize the project in a written instrument to be issued to the investor. Such instruments vary from country to country, and bear different names, including "investment agreement,"[1] "approval decree,"[2] "investment license," and "investment permit." Some may take the form of a detailed contract, while others may merely be a letter from the investment organization to the investor.

Despite variations, most host country authorizations may be analyzed as being either (1) an administrative act by the host country government concerned, or (2) a contract or agreement between the host country and the investor. Whether a particular authorization is analyzed as a contract or an administrative act may have implications for the enforceability of its provisions. Often, investment agreements contain provisions for international arbitration, or for dispute resolution by the International Center for Settlement of Investment Disputes,[3] an affiliate of the World Bank; consequently, such agreements may give the foreign investor greater assurance that the host country government will respect its provisions than would an authorization in the form of a "license" or "permit," which may, under local law, be modified at the will of the government. In some jurisdictions, investment approvals in the form of administrative acts may nonetheless afford the investor vested rights that are enforceable in the courts of law. In other jurisdictions, however, such administrative acts may be modified, or even abrogated unilaterally, at the will of the government. In any event, counsel for the investor should seek to determine the precise legal effect of any investment authorization under local law. In appropriate cases, counsel may wish to cast the results of his negotiations with the government in the form of an investment contract with reference to appropriate governing law and to international

---

[1] *See generally* Farer, *Economic Development Agreements: A Functional Analysis*, 10 Colum. J. Transnat'l Law 200–41 (1971).

[2] *See generally* Barringer, *Legal Aspects of Foreign Investment in Developing Countries*, in 4 *A Lawyer's Guide to International Business Transactions* 374 (W. Surrey & D. Wallace eds., 2d ed. 1980).

[3] *See* ch. 30, *Planning for Dispute Settlement in International Business Transactions*, and 31, *International Commercial Arbitration.*

§ 19.08

arbitration so as to limit the ability of the government to modify the terms of an agreement once made.

Normally the investment authorization, whether in the form of a contract or an administrative act, will contain, at the very minimum, provisions on repatriation of capital and income, foreign currency allocation for debt service and other foreign expenditures, a time schedule for the implementation of the project, permission for the project to import goods without payment of duty, the nature and extent of tax holidays and tax exemptions, requirements for submitting reports to the government, and other pertinent matters. More detailed investment agreements will also address such matters as training programs for employees, the number of permitted foreign employees, the ability of the government to use the project's facilities, and project procurement policies.[4]

Ordinarily, the host country will want to see that the project is underway as quickly as possible. The investor, on the other hand, will usually want to implement the project at its own pace. Most investment agreements and approvals include schedules which set deadlines for the implementation of the project. Failure to implement the project within the specified deadline will normally result in a revocation or cancellation of the authorization to undertake the investment; however, most investment laws permit the investor to seek extensions of such deadlines.

Some countries provide a procedure whereby a project may obtain provisional approval until such time as the feasibility study is completed and the necessary capital secured. Once the investor has definitely decided to undertake the project, it then applies for a permanent approval from the appropriate host country agency.

In a few instances, notably those concerning particularly important projects, the approval for the project may take the form of a decree of the Council of Ministers or the President, or even an act of the legislature.

---

[4] *See generally* Farer, *supra* n.1.

§ 19.09 Joint Ventures

In making a direct investment abroad, a company must make a strategic decision whether to undertake the project alone or in association with another business entity. If the investor decides to proceed alone, it must then decide whether the investment project will take the form of a branch or of a wholly-owned subsidiary. These two business forms are discussed in some detail in section 19.11, *infra*. If the investor decides to work with another business entity, its investment will take some form of a joint venture.

Prior to World War II, direct foreign investment normally took the form of a wholly-owned subsidiary in the host country. With the enormous expansion of international business in the postwar era, foreign investment has increasingly been cast in another form–the joint venture. Indeed, today, the joint venture is probably the most prevalent vehicle for undertaking a direct investment abroad.[1]

The term "joint venture" is used in a variety of ways and appears to have both general and specific definitions. In its most general sense, the joint venture, a form of business well known to American law,[2] is an association of two or more persons to undertake a relatively limited and well-defined business activity. Under U.S. law, a joint venture is essentially a partnership and, in most instances, is governed by partnership law.[3] In the realm of international business, the term "joint venture" has a variety of meanings. For some, it implies that the partners in a project have nationality different from one another or different from the country in which the joint venture is to operate. For example, the creation of a manufacturing facility in Canada by a French company and an American corporation would qualify as an "international joint venture." For many developing countries, the term has yet another meaning: it refers to an investment project in a host

---

[1] *See* Barringer, *Legal Aspects of Foreign Investment in Developing Countries*, in 4 A Lawyer's Guide to International Business Transactions 394.

[2] The joint venture was not recognized in English common law as a distinct legal entity, but began to be recognized as such in American courts in the latter half of the nineteenth century. American judges and lawyers have often referred to it as a "joint adventure." *See generally*, Mechem, *The Law of Joint Adventures*, 15 Minn. L. Rev. 644 (1931). *See also* Jaeger, *Joint Ventures: Origin, Nature and Development*, 9 Am. U.L. Rev. 1 (1960).

[3] *See* Z. Cavitch, 2 *Business Organizations* §§ 41.01–.02 (1981); A. Bromberg, *Crane and Bromberg on Partnership* § 35 (1968).

country by one or more foreigners and one or more *local* partners from the host country itself.[4] Among a few developing nations, it is used in an even more limited sense to mean a joint investment project in which at least one joint venture partner comes from the industrialized world, and at least one other partner is a local public enterprise from the host country itself.

As was indicated above, some host country laws require that a foreign investment project take the form of a such a joint venture, rather than a wholly owned subsidiary.

Whereas the term "joint venture" under U.S. law refers to a legal form of business enterprise either identical to or derived from a partnership,[5] its use within the context of international business does not connote a particular legal form of enterprise. Rather, the international joint venture is essentially an economic or financial relationship which may be cast into a variety of legal forms, depending upon the laws of the host country in question.

Analytically, international joint ventures can be divided into two categories: equity joint ventures and contractual joint ventures. The most common type, the equity joint venture, usually entails the creation of a separate joint venture legal entity in which each partner contributes capital to the venture and owns a portion of the resulting enterprise, while participating in its control and sharing its risks. In a contractual joint venture, the foreign partner, either by preference or because of the restrictions of local law, has no equity interest in an enterprise in the host country, but is merely obligated to provide certain services or operations on a long-term basis.[6] The variations on the contractual joint venture are numerous,[7] but in most instances the parties agree to undertake a particular business activity in which they may share profits and risks, while individually retaining ownership of any capital or assets necessary for the operation of the enterprise. For example, an American automobile manufacturer and

---

[4] *See* W. Friedmann & J. Beguin, *Joint International Business Ventures in Developing Countries* 3 (1971).

[5] A. Bromberg, *supra* n.3.

[6] *See id.* at 21–22. *See also* United Nations Industrial Development Organization (UNIDO), *Manual on the Establishment of Industrial Joint-Venture Agreements in Developing Countries* 3 (1971) [hereinafter cited as UNIDO].

[7] Barringer, *Legal Aspects of Foreign Investment in Developing Countries*, in 4 A Lawyer's Guide to International Business Transactions 401.

a Hungarian enterprise might agree to undertake jointly the manufacture of engines in Hungary at the Hungarian's plant, with the American providing the needed technology and marketing expertise, the Hungarian providing the factory, and both parties sharing expenses, as well as any profits, according to specified ratios.

In many instances, the foreign investor would prefer an equity, as opposed to a contractual joint venture, so as to obtain a long-term ownership interest in a profitable enterprise; however, where the profitability of the venture is questionable, the U.S. investor may instead favor a contractual, as opposed to an equity, joint venture, so as to avoid the risk of loss of capital. On the other hand, some countries may prohibit foreign investors from engaging in equity joint ventures altogether. Such may be the case in certain socialist countries whose laws require that the state own all means of production, or in mining and natural resource projects in developing countries, where the law vests ownership of all such resources exclusively in the state.

Numerous factors explain the enormous growth in joint ventures since World War II. One reason is that some host countries have required that foreign investment in their territories take this form rather than the form of a wholly-owned subsidiary. The degree and scope of this requirement vary from country to country. Some countries have adopted an absolute rule that prohibits all foreign investment unless it takes the form of a joint venture in which local investors–either public or private–own a majority of the equity and hold a controlling position. Others impose this requirement only in particularly important segments of the economy, such as agriculture, mining or natural resource development. Still others may require joint ventures as a general rule, but are willing to grant exceptions in appropriate cases.[8] In view of the variations in natural policies toward joint ventures, it is wise for the U.S. investor to determine the host country government's exact position on the question.

Several motives have prompted host countries to favor or even require joint ventures. One of the most important is the desire to integrate the investment project into the economy of the country. Host

---

[8] *E.g.*, Egypt's investment law, Law No. 43 of 1974, art. 4, provided that foreign investment projects are to "take the form of participation with public or private Egyptian capital . . .;" however, the Investment Authority was empowered to grant exceptions. *Investment Laws of the World* (Arab, Republic of Egypt, Text of Law) at 6.

government officials believe that with significant local participation, such integration is more likely to succeed than if the project is wholly-owned by foreigners. In addition, developing country governments consider that joint ventures facilitate the creation of local management skills and the transfer of technology, while mitigating the real or apparent foreign domination of the economy or important economic sectors. Joint ventures may also facilitate access by the local partner to the foreign partner's international marketing network. Moreover, it is argued that a joint venture, as opposed to a wholly-owned subsidiary, will be more responsive to government policies and conduct its operations in the best interests of the country as a whole. Finally, a joint venture places the host country government and the local investor in a position to take over the entire project through nationalization or negotiated purchase; consequently, its use is viewed as contributing to the formation of nationally-owned industries and economic activities.

Generally, investors have not shown great enthusiasm for the joint venture requirement due to a reluctance to share a potentially profitable venture, the fear of the difficulties that can arise from the divided management of an enterprise, and an unwillingness to reveal valuable technology which, in the end, may be used in competition against them.[9]

For this reason and in an effort to encourage foreign investment more actively, many countries have eliminated or eased the joint venture requirements since the late 1980s as they undertook the process of transformation from command to market economies and became more active in their pursuit of foreign capital.

At the same time, one finds that multinational corporations on their own initiative have increasingly turned to joint ventures or "strategic alliances" as an important tool of international business activity. They have preferred the joint venture to the wholly owned subsidiary in numerous situations—when they seek to share the risks of a venture, to obtain needed capital which they are unable or unwilling to contribute, to penetrate the markets by using the expertise and marketing organization of the partner, or to obtain needed technology and know-how which they do not possess. Moreover, when local interests are involved in a project, a joint venture may present fewer

---

[9] Travaglini, *Foreign Licensing and Joint Venture Arrangements*, in *Foreign Business Practices* 83 (U.S. Dept. of Commerce, 1981).

political risks and be less susceptible to nationalization than would a company owned entirely by foreigners.

On occasion, certain foreign investors have actually advocated joint ventures as a way of doing business. For example, at the height of the petro-dollar surplus in the oil-producing states of the Middle East during the mid-and late 1970's, numerous western firms were actively seeking to organize "trilateral ventures" in developing countries, a form of joint venture which would bring together western technology, Arab capital, and local resources and manpower in a single project.[10] Often, western companies will purport to enter into a joint venture as a means of selling their technology and products to the host country. In such cases, the western firm makes a small contribution to capital—often in the form of capitalized technology—and then enters into long-term, lucrative contracts to sell its equipment, technology, management services, and technical assistance to the joint venture in question, which is almost wholly-financed by the host country.

The organization of a joint venture will ordinarily require the expenditure of more time and funds than does the organization of a wholly-owned subsidiary, since the U.S. investor must first engage in a sometimes lengthy search for an appropriate partner, and then undertake protracted negotiations in order to define the relationship that is to exist among the parties to the joint venture. The search for an appropriate joint venture partner often encounters the same types of problems faced in identifying an appropriate foreign distributor.[11] In many countries—often, ironically, those which require joint ventures as a condition for investment—the U.S. investor may find that few, if any, local enterprises have the necessary experience and financial resources to become useful and reliable joint venture partners. Sometimes, U.S. companies have turned to their reliable foreign distributors, representatives or licensees to find satisfactory partners.

Yet, in many countries where the private sector is underdeveloped, or indeed non-existent, a government-owned enterprise, a ministry, or a publicly-financed development bank may afford the U.S. investor the only realistic possibilities for finding a local joint venture partner in the host country. As was indicated in section 1.04 [C] *supra*,

---

[10] Salacuse, *Arab Capital and Trilateral Ventures in the Middle East: Is Three a Crowd?*, in *Rich and Poor States in the Middle East* 129–163 (Kerr & Yassine, eds. 1982).

[11] *See* § 11.04, *supra*.

international business relationships with such entities may present peculiar problems. For example, whereas the goal of the U.S. investor is usually the maximization of profit, a public enterprise may pursue social objectives or national development. This divergence of basic objectives may eventually provoke conflict within the joint venture; for example, in times of slow demand, the U.S. partner might seek to reduce the labor force to cut costs, while the public enterprise partner might insist on retaining idle labor so as not to increase unemployment in the country. Additional conflict may be engendered by decisions on pricing the venture's products and services, allocating contracts for the supply of materials from local or foreign contractors, and training host country personnel. In addition to such business problems, joint ventures with foreign public entities may pose certain special legal issues, such as possible claims of sovereign immunity in the event of a legal dispute. Normally, counsel to the U.S. investor may avoid this problem by securing a waiver of foreign sovereign immunity from the public enterprise and by providing for the arbitration of disputes under the auspices of some neutral international body.[12]

---

[12] Normally in jurisdictions adopting the restrictive theory of foreign sovereign immunity, a governmental enterprise engaged in commercial activity is not entitled to the protection of sovereign immunity in respect of suits arising out of such activity. For example, most of the joint ventures discussed here would not be accorded such immunity under the Foreign Sovereign Immunities Act of 1976, 28 U.S.C. §§ 1330, 1391, 1602–1611. Some issues such as determining the nature of "commercial activity" are not fully settled, however. As a result, counsel to investors may wish to include a waiver of immunity clause in the joint venture agreement as an aid to enforcement of the investor's rights against a foreign state or instrumentality. Following is an example of such a clause:

The (*foreign or state entity*) hereby irrevocably waives any immunity to which it might otherwise be entitled now or in the future in any action or proceedings in any court of general jurisdiction, within or outside its territory, with respect to this Agreement, from jurisdiction and from the execution or enforcement of any judgment or other relief obtained in such an action or proceedings, including attachment prior to judgment for the purpose of securing satisfaction of any judgment that has been or may be entered against the (foreign state or entity.

Carl, *Suing Foreign Governments in American Courts: the United States Foreign Sovereign Immunities Act in Practice*, 33 Sw. L.J. 1009, 1055–56 (1979). *See generally id.*; von Mehren, *The Foreign Sovereign Immunities Act of 1976*, 17 Colum. J. Transnat'l L. 33 (1978). For a more detailed discussion of sovereign immunity, arbitration, and settlement of disputes generally, see ch. 30, *Planning for Dispute Settlement in International Business Transactions*, 31, *International Commercial Arbitration*, and 32, *Foreign Governments as Parties to Disputes*.

On occasion, a public entity may prove to be an effective joint venture partner by virtue of its political power. For example, a public enterprise may be better equipped than a private sector partner to secure local financing, necessary government approvals, and needed foreign exchange allocations from the Central Bank.

In addition to local partners, whether public or private, certain international organizations and agencies may participate in the joint venture with the U.S. investor. The International Finance Corporation,[13] the Arab Investment Company,[14] and the InterAmerican Development Bank,[15] among others, may provide financing or contribute equity to ventures in which U.S. businesses are involved. These agencies also have their own particular objectives and methods of operation.

In virtually every case, the joint venturers will seek to embody their relationship in a written joint venture agreement. Because of the divergence of objectives and perspectives among the potential partners—local, foreign, and international—the negotiation of the joint venture agreement may take considerable time and will demand great negotiating skill from all parties concerned.[16]

---

[13] *See* § 4.04[C], *supra.*

[14] *See* § 4.05[D], *supra.*

[15] *See* § 4.05[A], *supra.*

[16] For a general discussion of negotiating techniques, see ch. 1, *supra. See* generally, Salacuse, Making Global Deals—What Every Executive Should Know About Negotiating Abroad (1991). See Shelp, *Dealing With Host Country Governments as Co-Venturers or Otherwise: How to Maximize the Good and Minimize the Bad, or "How to Negotiate with Latin American Governments"*, in Current Legal Aspects of Doing Business in Latin America 157–80 (S. Stairs ed. 1981).

§ 19.10 Joint Venture Agreements

[A] Joint Venture Negotiating Process

Negotiating a joint venture abroad requires a mastery of both the *substance* and the *process* of the transaction. Business negotiators sometimes become so enmeshed in substantive issues that they forget or neglect effective management of the process of creating the deal. Without neglecting such important substantive issues as capital contributions, management structure, and guarantees, joint venture negotiators must also constantly bear in mind the negotiating process—the progressive movement toward a desired end.

For some lawyers, the process of negotiation is essentially one of compromise, of striking a deal somewhere in the middle between their initial offering point and that of their counterpart. For others, negotiating a deal is combat, a means to dominate a business opponent, to assert their will over an adversary. In the area of international business transactions, particularly *long-term deals*, such as joint ventures, negotiators should consider adopting yet another, perhaps more neutral definition: negotiation is a process by which two or more persons interact to advance individual interests through joint action. Joint action requires agreement between the parties concerned, and negotiation is the means to attain that agreement. In this perspective, negotiating an international business transaction is essentially a search for the joint interests of the parties and for legal structures to accommodate those interest.

[B] The Phases of a Negotiation

Like other processes, a joint venture negotiation tends to go through distinct phases. The effective negotiator understands those phases and recognizes that each calls for distinct skills, approaches, and resources. Virtually all negotiations tend to pass through three basic phases:

[1] Prenegotiation

In the first phase, which can be called prenegotiation, the parties to a potential deal determine whether they want to negotiate at all and, if they do, what they will negotiate about, and how, when, and where they will go about it. Much of prenegotiation may happen in letters, telephone calls, and faxes, even before the parties sit down together, but it may continue for many meetings thereafter. This phase is characterized by information-gathering and efforts by each of the parties to evaluate the other. It ends when both sides make a decision to negotiate a deal with the other, or when one informs the other, directly or indirectly, that it no longer wishes to continue discussions.

As a general rule, Asians tend to devote more time and attention to the prenegotiation phase of joint venture negotiations than do Americans. Whereas American executives and lawyers generally want to "dispense with the preliminaries" and "to get down to cases", most Asians view prenegotiation as an essential foundation to any business relationship; consequently they recognize the need to conduct prenegotiation with care before actually making a decision to undertake substantive negotiations of a deal. One of the consequences of this difference in approach is that Americans sometimes assume that discussions with Asian counterparts have passed from prenegotiation to a subsequent stage when in fact they have not because the Asians have not yet decided to undertake substantive negotiations. This type of misunderstanding can lead to suspicions of bad faith, resulting ultimately in total failure of the talks. It is therefore important to be sure that you and your counterparts are always in the same phase of the deal-making process. One way of making sure is by using written agendas, memoranda, and letters of intent to mark the various phases.

[a] Confidentiality and Exchange of Information Agreements

Neither party may be able to make a decision to enter into negotiations with the other without exchanging confidential information relating to their respective technologies, business plans, financial resources, and other sensitive matters. On the one hand, the information disclosed should be sufficiently explicit to allow the parties to decide whether they want to enter into a joint venture relationship. On the other hand, it should not be so extensive as to give the parties a valuable resource to use other than for intended purposes. Should negotiations fail, the use of such exchanged information by one of the parties thereafter could be damaging to the other. Once a potential joint venture partner has been identified, it is therefore common for the parties to enter into an Information Exchange Agreement or a Confidentiality Agreement to protect information that may be exchanged during the course of the negotiation.

Such an agreement must first obligate each of the parties to preserve the confidentiality of information exchanged and not to disclose it to any third party without the written consent of the party originally disclosing it in the negotiation. It should also bind the party receiving such information to use care in limiting, selecting and contractually bindings the personnel to whom it gives access to the confidential information. In general, the dissemination of the information to employees should be on a need to know basis. The Agreement might also contain prohibitions on the reproduction of any documents exchanged and a an explicit contractual obligation to return any confidential information and all copies thereof to the original disclosing party. And finally, it is common in such Confidentiality or Exchange of Information Agreements to include an explicit provision that no right or license, expressed or implied, is granted to the receiving party to use the confidential information other than in the manner and to the extent stated by the Agreement itself.

[2] Conceptualization

In the second phase of the process, which might be called conceptualization, the parties seek to agree on a basic concept or formula upon which to build their deal. They attempt to establish the fundamental principles that will govern their future business relationship. For example, are they to undertake and equity or a contractual joint venture? In manufacturing, are they seeking to establish a joint venture to which both will contribute capital or will one of the parties provide technology only? Once the parties have agreed on the basic nature of their transaction, they will then need to find an acceptable formula for its structure. For example, in one case involving the renegotiation of a long-term contract for the sale of electricity between a government-owned power company and foreign-owned aluminum smelter, the parties, who were stymied on the question of price, only made process when they agreed on the formula that the price of electricity under the contract would be "linked to the international price of energy."

The conceptualization phase of negotiations is marked by the parties' definition of their interests, the advancement of proposals and counter proposals, and the exploration of options. Here the creativity of negotiators comes into play, as they seek to shape a basic concept and to find a formula for their deal that will allow both sides to benefit and satisfy their interests. Once the parties have agreed on a formula, they may sign a letter of intent or similar document to memorialize their understanding.

[a] Letter of Intent or Memorandum of Understanding

Neither a letter of intent nor a memorandum of understanding is legally required to complete a joint venture. These documents serve basically to record the intentions of the parties and their fundamental understanding up to that point in the negotiations. They may also enable each of the potential joint venture partners to obtain the necessary internal corporate authorizations to pursue subsequent phases of the joint venture negotiations. They also serve to provide momentum and a sense of accomplishment to the negotiations themselves. Normally, they set out the general structure of the proposed venture; however, they should make clear that the stated intentions or understandings are nothing more than a basis for further negotiations and, in the event the parties do not reach agreement, for whatever reason, neither party will be liable to the other. In some cases, a letter of intent or memorandum of understanding may provide for some degree of liability (e.g., expenses incurred in the negotiation process), but strictly limit the extent of that liability. If timing is important, the memorandum or letter should state a deadline for completing the negotiations or the various actions need to launch the joint venture. And finally, the letter or agreement might include an "exclusivity" provision" providing that neither party will conduct negotiations with any third party for a similar joint venture without notice to the other.

[3] Detail Arrangement

The final phase in the joint venture negotiation process is devoted to working out the details and implications of the agreed upon formula. This phase relies heavily on technical expertise as the parties explore and attempt to solve the problems of implementation. Here, the parties may come to understand the full meaning of the old saying "the devil is in the details" as they face the frustration of making their formula "work" and as they seek to overcome numerous minor difficulties that assume major proportions, that seem to have the potential to become "deal killers." For example, it is one thing to agree to a formula that the price of electricity should be linked to the international price of energy, it is quite another to turn that formula is to an effective pricing system that can be applied day to day throughout the life of the deal. The challenge for the lawyer is to document these various understandings on details into a definitive joint venture contract and related agreements that will govern the business relationship of the parties involved.

§ 19.10[B] INTERNATIONAL PLANNING 19–92

No negotiation is neat as this tripartite analysis would suggest.[1] After prenegotiation, the parties may discuss details before arriving at a formula, instead of agreeing on a formula first. Then, too, the point at which one phase ends and another begins may be difficult to determine with any precision. In many cases, however, the end of one phase may be clearly marked by the preparation of a document. Thus, the prenegotiation phase may end with a memorandum or agenda setting a time, place, and subject matter for negotiation; the conceptualization phase may finish with the preparation of a letter of intent or memorandum of understanding; and the details phase concludes with the signature of a final contract.

As will be seen in section 19.11, *infra*, the parties will normally cast their joint venture in a particular legal form of enterprise under the laws of the host country, and in most instances, it will take the form of a company or corporation. Prior to that stage, however, the parties must engage in lengthy negotiations in order to arrive at a definitive, written joint venture agreement which defines their relationship in detail. The joint venture agreement may be embodied in a single document; however, in most instances, it consists of several agreements—a basic joint venture contract sometimes called a "founders agreement," and individual, auxiliary agreements covering such matters as management services, patent and trademark licensing, technical services, loans, and long-term sales arrangements. Appendices 19A and 19B to the present chapter contain examples of joint venture agreements governing the development and operation of a sugar plantation and refinery.

Joint venture agreements are by no means standard, and their provisions vary according to the intentions and the needs of the parties.[2] While one cannot set down in these pages a definite formula for drafting joint venture agreements, it should be noted that the legislation or regulations of the host country may require that the agreement treat particular issues in a prescribed fashion.

The preparation of the final joint venture agreement may proceed in stages. Before binding themselves to a definitive joint venture

---

[1] For a discussion of this tripartite analysis, see Zartman & Berman, The Practical Negotiator (1982). *See also*, Salacuse, Making Global Deals—What Every Executive Should Know About Negotiating Abroad 23-27 (1992).

[2] *See* United Nations Industrial Development Organization (UNIDO), Manual on the Establishment of Industrial Joint-Venture Agreements in Developing Countries 1 (1971) [hereinafter cited as UNIDO].

contract, the parties might first conclude a preliminary agreement to undertake a feasibility study of the proposed project, to explore the modes of financing it, and to determine other essential issues within a fixed period of time. If, upon satisfaction of these conditions, the parties remain convinced of the desirability of the project, they may then proceed to negotiate and conclude a definitive joint venture agreement, along with other necessary contracts. As will be seen from the documents included in the Appendices to this chapter, the evolution of the Agrarian Sugar Company took place in two such stages.

The agreement itself may be as detailed and as complex as the parties require in order to obtain their objectives. While no standard form exists, most joint ventures will treat certain basic issues. They include the following:

[C] Recitals

The joint venture contract will ordinarily begin with a recital by the parties of their past dealings with one another, their intentions in undertaking the project, and the circumstances under which they have reached their agreement. In the event of any future conflict on matters not specifically covered in the agreement itself, the recitals may be useful, as statements of intention, in negotiations or in arbitration aimed at resolving such dispute.

[D] Organization and Capitalization

The agreement will normally specify in some detail the capital to be contributed by each of the parties and the steps to be taken to establish the contemplated joint venture company. Normally, it will provide for the type of legal form to be used, the law under which it is to be organized, and the party or parties who will have the responsibility for fulfilling the legal requirements of the organization and for obtaining other necessary government approvals. The agreement will stipulate the authorized capital, how the shares are to be allocated among the parties, and the time when each party is to make its capital contribution. It should be recalled, however, that host country legislation may impose a maximum limitation on the percentage of ownership allowed to foreigners.

In addition, if other forms of financing are contemplated, such as loans or export credits, and the parties have an obligation either to provide, guarantee, or procure them from other persons, the joint venture agreement should also stipulate those responsibilities. If the contribution to capital is to be paid in cash, the agreement must precisely specify the type of currency in which payment is to be made. Normally, both the foreign and local partners will want to limit their capital exposure by holding cash equity payments to a minimum; consequently, debt/equity ratios of joint ventures are usually high. If the contributions are to be made in property or technology, the agreement should contain specific provisions concerning the valuation of such non-cash contributions. Difficult problems concerning the relative value of contributions by foreign and local partners can arise when the government maintains an artificially high exchange rate which has the effect of overvaluing host country currency and assets.

Yet another problem which the parties should address at this stage concerns capital contribution for future expansion of the project. Sometimes the local partner will be unwilling or unable to make such contribution at the appropriate time, and the entire burden will fall on the foreign partner, in which case the parties will be forced to resolve the difficult issues of adjusting the relative ownership shares and control to correspond fairly to total capital contributions.

[E] Pre-incorporation Expenses

Certain parties to the joint venture may have incurred significant pre-incorporation expenses for such matters as feasibility studies, engineering designs, legal fees, and travel. The agreement will often stipulate how those pre-incorporation expenses are to be borne. One possibility is, of course, that the contemplated joint venture company, once formed, will reimburse the parties in cash for those expenses. Another possibility is to capitalize the expenses and include them as the party's contribution to capital for which it will receive shares. On the other hand, the parties may agree that each will bear its own costs, as is reasonable for any investor to do in investigating a possible investment.

[F] Control and Management

In view of the potential differences in the objectives and attitudes of joint venture partners, the creation of a satisfactory control structure for the venture is imperative. Toward this end, the agreement will contain various control provisions which will also be included in the articles of incorporation or the bylaws of the proposed company. Among the issues to be treated in the agreement are the size of the board of directors, the manner in which the various parties will be represented thereon, the election of directors, the procedures of the board, and the selection of officers. Where the board of directors is large, the joint venturers may find it appropriate to create a special executive committee to which the board may delegate powers concerning the ongoing execution of the project. Such a device may be particularly convenient to obviate the need for extensive foreign travel by numerous persons to attend regular meetings of the full board of directors. The sample agreement in Appendix 19A adopts this approach.

In view of potential divergences in objectives and strategies between the local partner and the foreign partner, control is a particularly difficult issue to resolve in formulating the joint venture agreement. The minority partner is normally unwilling to leave its fate entirely to the will of the majority, and it will therefore seek to write special protective provisions into the agreement. The thrust of such provisions is to give the minority partner a veto over major decisions with which it may not agree. This result is most often achieved by requiring a super-majority, or even unanimity, for board action over especially important issues. The danger of such an approach is, of course, that the enterprise may be thrown into a state of paralysis in the event of a protracted conflict among the partners.

In many joint ventures, shares are evenly divided between the partners. Here, depending on the original will and foresight of the parties, the control structure may be organized in such a way as to insure deadlock and inaction in the event of disagreement, or preferably to provide a means by which the deadlock may ultimately be broken, as through the use of various devices such as granting a tie-breaking vote to an independent member of the board, informal dispute resolution procedures, arbitration, delegation ultimate authority on ceratin specified issues, and buy-sell options.

In a joint venture with host country partners, the foreign partner, even though contributing only a small portion of the capital, will ordinarily seek to assure itself a position from which it will be able to "run" the joint venture. Since it is ordinarily supplying technology, management, and marketing, the foreign partner usually believes that it cannot provide these elements effectively or protect its proprietary technology adequately unless it dominates the operation of the enterprise. One means of divorcing management from ownership to achieve this result is for the joint venture to enter into a long-term management contract (see § 12.08 and Appendix 12B, *supra*) with the foreign partner, who will then have responsibility for the day-to-day operation of the venture.

Whether or not a separate management contract is negotiated, the joint venture agreement must treat in detail the appointment and removal of the executive officers and those charged with the general management of the project. In joint ventures in which the partners are equal participants, it is common for one partner to appoint the chairman of the board of directors and the other to designate the president or chief executive officer. The provisions on these matters must be coordinated with any special management services agreement between the joint venture company and an outside manager. As was indicated in Chapter 12, *supra*, it is essential to define the relationship between the Board and the outside manager since the potential for conflict between them is great. And finally, since one of the host country's objectives in entering into a joint venture is to facilitate the transfer of management skills, the joint venture agreement might also include a definite schedule for the development of local managerial expertise, as well as a statement of the obligations of the foreign partner to train local persons.

[G] Financial Policies

The parties ought to reach some basic agreement on the financial principles governing the joint venture. While this subject covers numerous issues, perhaps one of the most difficult concerns the distribution of profits. If the venture becomes profitable, severe conflict may arise over whether profits should be distributed to the partners or retained for the expansion of the enterprise. Often foreign partners seek the latter, while local partners desire the former. Consequently, to avoid dangerous conflicts over this issue, the joint venture agreement should stipulate some basic principles to govern the distribution of profits. For example, it might provide that before any profits of the joint venture company shall be distributed as dividends to the shareholders, a stipulated percentage of each year's net after-tax profits shall be set aside to meet the capital and other requirements of the joint company.[3] In negotiating this provision, the local partner will, of course, be fully aware that the foreign partner

---

[3] UNIDO, *supra* n.2, at 27.

has numerous means besides dividend payments to extract profits from the enterprise, including management contracts and technology transfer agreements.

[H] Other Obligations and Guarantees

The joint venture agreement should state clearly any obligations and guarantees which the parties in their individual capacities have agreed to undertake for, or on behalf of, the joint venture. Thus, if the government is a party to the agreement and has agreed to provide tax incentives, assistance in the construction of infrastructure, subsidized loans, and other privileges and immunities, the agreement should clearly state the nature of such obligations. If the government is not a party to the contract, the joint venturers, in appropriate cases, may seek to have it recognized or acknowledged by the government, so as to have some assurance that the government will not interfere with it at some time in the future.

On the other hand, the local partner may seek, and local law may require, that the foreign partner, especially if it is supplying technology and know-how, guarantee its quality–and even the results to be achieved–through its application. In such cases, the foreign party may be able to negotiate limits to such liability and perhaps obtain insurance locally to cover the risk.[4]

[I] Auditors and Accounting

The agreement should stipulate basic provisions with respect to auditing the joint venture's operations–provisions essential to the protection of the interests of the parties and to the preservation of harmony in their continuing relationships. Since the accounting profession in certain third world countries may not be developed nor fully capable of working on the complex audits of such enterprises, joint venture agreements often provide that the auditor must be acceptable to all the partners and be an internationally-recognized accounting firm. In the alternative, the agreement may specifically appoint a named firm of auditors in order to limit future discretion with regard to this important matter.

[J] Transfer of Shares

Because the relationships among joint venture partners are usually crucial to the success of the enterprise, the agreement will normally

---
[4] Flynn, *Anatomy of a Yugoslav Joint Venture*, Int'l Fin. L. Rev. 7, 9 (August 1982).

contain provisions governing the transfer of shares to third persons, as well as changes in the relative equity positions of the parties. In most cases, such shares will not be freely transferrable, but instead, subject to the approval of the other parties. Moreover, the agreement may provide for some sort of buy-sell arrangement to enable the parties to liquidate their investment under certain conditions, for example, only after a period of years, or only if the venture attains a certain level of profitability. Valuation provisions are, of course, essential to such an arrangement. In drafting such provisions, counsel should not forget that local law may limit the maximum amount of equity participation which foreigners may own in projects.

[K] Dispute Settlement and Applicable Law

As in most international business agreements, the joint venture agreement should stipulate the applicable law, and provide for the settlement of disputes–normally by international arbitration. In view of the fact that preservation of cordial relationships among the partners is ordinarily essential to the enterprise, it is often provided that parties must engage in good faith negotiation and conciliation before invoking formal arbitration.[5]

[L] Termination

Joint ventures often tend to be unstable, and they may terminate for many reasons, including achievement of the purposes for which they were formed, fundamental disagreement among the parties, basic changes in the law or business conditions that make continuation unfeasible or illegal, management deadlock, change in control of one of the partners, or bankruptcy. The joint venture should specify the events that will trigger termination and the consequences flowing therefrom. A termination provision may provide for the liquidation and dissolution of the joint venture entity or for its continuation by one or more of the joint venture partners. In either case, the joint venture should specify the consequences of termination with respect to division of assets and liabilities of the joint venture, indemnifications, discharges, payment of outstanding loans that have been guaranteed by joint venture partners, the return of all confidential information and materials and the continuation of confidentiality

---

[5] For a discussion of this subject, see ch. 30, *Planning for Dispute Settlement in International Business Transactions*.

obligations, and arrangements with respect to licensing or assignment of technology rights.

§ 19.11 The Legal Form of the Investment Project

[A] Choosing Between a Branch and a Subsidiary

Undertaking a direct investment in a foreign country will necessitate a decision on the legal form which the investment project is to take. At the outset, the investor must determine whether the project will be either a branch or an independently-organized subsidiary. A branch is an integral part of the company undertaking the investment, and it usually constitutes a presence by such company in the host country. A subsidiary, on the other hand, is legally independent of the parent and is organized as a separate entity, normally as a corporation under the laws of the host country.

Numerous factors will affect the decision as to whether to establish the project as a branch or a subsidiary. A summary checklist of such factors is to be found in Appendix 11C *supra*. Among the most important of these considerations are the tax consequences of the choice under the laws of both the host country and the investor's home country. Chapter 21 *infra*, will consider the tax issues of the question at great length.[1]

Other aspects of local law will also have a major influence on the decision. For example, the legislation of the host country may specifically forbid the use of a branch in establishing a foreign investment project, or it may indirectly make a subsidiary the only realistic organizational form available to the investor, as in the case, for example, where the host country investment code grants incentives only to companies incorporated under local law. Moreover, if local law requires that investment projects take the form of a joint venture, the use of a separately-incorporated subsidiary may be the only realistic means of satisfying that requirement.

Since a branch constitutes the presence of the investor in the host country, and thereby at least theoretically exposes all of its assets to host country jurisdiction, the investor may prefer to avoid such result by incorporating the investment project as a separate subsidiary. In addition, the investor may choose to form a subsidiary under local law in order to reduce somewhat the foreign image of the investment

---

[1] For a summary analysis of the tax consequences of establishing a manufacturing plant as a branch or a subsidiary in eleven different countries, see generally *Methods of Organizing a Foreign Business,* in 3 The Tax Management International Forum 3-40 (March 1982, no. 1).

project and give it a more local appearance. A further factor affecting the decision will be the cost and formalities required for conducting business in the two possible forms. Traditionally, branches could be established with a minimum of cost; however, today the establishment of a branch in many countries may require expense and formalities as onerous as those needed for organizing a separately-incorporated subsidiary. For example, if a foreign company wishes to conduct business as a branch in Mexico, it must obtain the approval of the Department of National Economy, and it must also register in the public commercial registry. The satisfaction of both requirements necessitates the preparation and submission of significant documentation.[2] Moreover, once established, a Mexican branch must publish an annual balance sheet that has been approved by a certified public accountant.

In practice, except in banking and mining, the vast majority of foreign investment projects take the form of a subsidiary, rather than a branch, of the investor;[3] consequently, the remainder of this section will be devoted to an examination of the organization of a subsidiary.

[B] The Organization of the Subsidiary

In theory, the investor seeking to establish a subsidiary may do so under the law of the host country, the law of his home country, or the law of some third country. In practice, legal and tax considerations may limit the scope of the choice. For example, the host country may require that investment projects on its territory take the form of a subsidiary organized under its own legislation.

The American investor who organizes a subsidiary under the laws of a foreign country will often find that the rules and principles governing the formation, operation, and dissolution of such entity differ significantly from those governing business organizations in the United States. Ordinarily, the U.S. investor will find certain similarities with business enterprises in countries sharing the common law heritage—such as England, Canada, and Australia–but even here, despite significant similarities, he will also encounter notable differences from American law. On the other hand, in the numerous countries of the world that have been influenced by the civil law

---

[2] Southern Methodist University, 1 *Doing Business in Mexico* at § 29.02.

[3] *See* Young, *Establishing and Financing a Foreign Enterprise*, 1976 Tax Mgmt. Int'l J. 76–11 at 14, 15.

tradition,[4] the American business person and his lawyer will discover that the law of business organizations presents numerous unfamiliar concepts, principles, rules, and procedures. Consequently, any survey of the law of business enterprises throughout the world must begin by dividing the globe into those countries, such as England, Nigeria, and India, whose business entities have been influenced by the English common law tradition, and those countries, such as France, Germany, and Egypt, whose business organizations have been influenced by civil law.

Generally speaking, countries having a common law heritage offer the investor essentially two forms of enterprise from which to choose: the partnership and the company. In virtually all instances, the investor will choose the company since, like the American corporation, it provides its shareholders with limited liability, facilitates centralized management of the enterprise, and exists as a distinct legal entity. Normally, a separate statute called a "Companies Act," or "Companies Law," governs the formation and operation of such an entity.[5] Unlike most American laws which have traditionally recognized only one legal form of corporation,[6] regardless of size or number of investors, company laws following the English model recognize two forms: (i) the public company, which may sell its shares to the public and have them publicly traded, and (ii) the private company, which may not. This distinction, which has its origins in the English Companies (Consolidation) Act of 1908, is designed to provide one form of company for enterprises which raise capital from the public, and another form for small businesses which want a separate legal personality, but which do not issue securities publicly.[7] The former are subject to special rules to protect the public, while the latter are not. Until recently, a private company under English law was one whose articles (a) restricted the right to transfer shares; (b) limited its membership to fifty shareholders, with certain exceptions, and (c) prohibited the company from making any invitation to the public to subscribe to its shares or debentures. A company not complying with

---

[4] *See* § 1.04[A], *supra*.

[5] Examples of countries whose company laws have been shaped by the English common law tradition are: United Kingdom; Canada; Australia; Nigeria; New Zealand; the Sudan; and India.

[6] Many states have departed from this tradition through the enactment of "close corporation" statutes.

[7] Gower, *Company Law* 13, 299 (4th ed. 1979).

these requirements was automatically considered public. Recently, as a result of EEC directives designed to harmonize United Kingdom company legislation with that of the other member states in the European Community, the definition has undergone a significant modification to sharpen the distinction between the two, including the addition of a high minimum capital requirement for public companies; however, it freed private companies from the requirement of share restrictions and from limitations on the number of members, while maintaining the prohibition on public offerings. Nonetheless, while the law in England itself has undergone significant change, the old definition may still be in effect in countries influenced by English company law.[8]

The partnership, which is normally governed by a distinct "Partnership Act" in most common law jurisdictions, would not normally provide an effective vehicle for most investment projects—except for certain types of joint ventures—since it subjects the partners to joint and several liability, and does not constitute a separate legal entity. On the other hand, in certain cases, it may offer significant advantages, including the absence of required government approvals for formation, no minimum capital and registration requirements, and rapid and inexpensive procedures of organization.[9]

In countries having a European civil law tradition, the foreign investor appears to confront a greater variety of legal forms of enterprise than he does in common law countries. Most publications on "doing business abroad" delight in listing them; however, upon close examination, the choice is not as great as it appears. The name given to each of the various forms of enterprises in civil law countries normally include the foreign language equivalent of the word "company,"—the "*société*" in French-speaking jurisdictions, *societa* in Italian, *sociedad* in Spanish-speaking areas, *Gesellschaft* in German, or the *Sharika* in the Arabic-speaking regions of the world. In these countries, the "company" is the basic legal concept upon which all of the law of business enterprises is built. Thus, corporations and partnerships, associations and limited partnerships, are all considered forms of the "company."

---

[8] *See* Gore-Brown *On Companies* 7–2 (43rd ed.).

[9] For a series of articles analyzing the advantages and disadvantages of using the partnership as opposed to the corporation in undertaking investment in various European countries, see generally 8 Int'l Bus. L. 317 (1980).

Normally, the Civil Code will set down certain basic principles concerning companies. For example, Article 1832 of the French Civil Code, defines a "company" (societe) as "an agreement of two or more persons to put something in common with the view to sharing the resulting profits." The *societe* includes both corporations and partnerships, enterprises which the Anglo-American law has tended to treat as two distinct and unrelated forms.[10] Accordingly, the law of France, as well as of many countries which have been inspired by French legislation, provides for five types of commercial companies: *the société en nom collectif*, which corresponds to the American partnership; *the société en commandite simple* which corresponds to the limited partnership; *the société à responsabilité limitée*, a private limited company which exists as a distinct form; *the société anonym*, which corresponds to the public corporation; and *the société en commandite par actions*, which corresponds to the joint stock company. Unlike Anglo-American law, some civil law jurisdictions consider the partnership to constitute a distinct legal person; however, even in such jurisdictions, its members, like partners of an American partnership, do not enjoy limited liability.

Despite the array of "companies" which seem to confront the investor under host country law, in practice there exist fewer options than initially appear. In most instances, the investor is seeking a legal form of enterprise which corresponds more or less to the American corporation—that is, a form which constitutes a distinct legal entity, grants its shareholders limited liability, permits centralization of management, offers the possibility of perpetual, or at least long life, and permits the transfer of shares, at least in certain limited circumstances. Consequently, in most host countries, the investor really has a choice between only two distinct business forms: the equivalent of the closed corporation, or the equivalent of a company whose shares are potentially marketable.

Most countries having a European civil law tradition provide two distinct legal forms governed by separate statutes: a form which is designed for the closely-held company, and another form which is designed for those companies whose shares will be publicly sold. The former, often referred to in English as the "limited liability company," or "private limited company," originated in Germany in 1892 with

---

[10] *Amos and Walton's Introduction to French Law* 346 (Lawson, Anton & Brown 3rd ed. 1969).

a law to establish the *Gesellschaft mit beschrankter Haftung* (commonly known as the G.m.b.H). It spread throughout most of Europe and to many non-European areas; it is known today in French as the *société à responsabilité limitée*, and in Spanish as the *sociedad de responsabilidad limitada*.

The second form of company, which allows the public sale of its shares, and is often referred to in English as the "public company" or the "stock company," is known in French as the *société anonyme*, in German as the *Aktien Gesellschaft*, and in Spanish as the *sociedad anónima*. Each form has its own particular characteristics, and is governed by distinct legislation. The distinction between the two forms is based on the assumption that a business enterprise which seeks capital from the public, and which has numerous shareholders who are not actually engaged in the management of the business, ought to be subjected to a different set of rules than an enterprise which consists of a few owners who actively participate in the business. As noted above, English law also recognizes this distinction.

As a practical matter, the investor contemplating a subsidiary in most civil law countries will be required to choose between these two forms of the company. Obviously, if the project contemplates the mobilization of capital from the public through the sale of shares, the investor will be required to organize a public company, since the private company is by its very nature forbidden to sell shares to the public, or to allow its shares to be freely traded. Moreover, the laws of some countries prohibit the use of one form or the other in specific types of business activities. For example, the French S.A.R.L. may not be used for enterprises in insurance and banking; however, the law requires that a real estate management company must be a S.A.R.L. On the other hand, if the project does not contemplate the sale of shares to the public, the investor may nonetheless decide to use the public company form for other reasons. For example, in Mexico, foreign investors tend more often to organize their projects in the form of a *sociedad anónima*, rather than a *sociedad de responsabilidad limitada*, despite the fact that the project will be wholly-owned by the parent and that no public subscription of shares is contemplated.

While the American lawyer is used to thinking that all corporations are governed by the same legal rules, he or she should be aware that in many countries of the world the rules governing the private company and the public company are different, and that the decision to organize in one form or the other may have significant implications for the future operation of the investment project. Consequently, the prudent American investor should seek the advice of local counsel in choosing the appropriate legal form for the subsidiary.

[C] Issues in the Organization of a Foreign Company

In organizing a company under the laws of a foreign country, the U.S. investor will encounter a host of unfamiliar requirements and procedures. The limited space available in this section does not permit even a summary of the company and corporate laws prevailing throughout the world; consequently, this section will limit its discussion to certain general issues normally faced in establishing an investment in the form of a company under the laws of the host country. It will tend to emphasize those common foreign legal requirements which normally are not found in American corporation laws. The bibliography at the end of this chapter contains a list of English-language publications treating the corporate laws of particular countries.

As indicated above, most governments normally exercise some control over the establishment of a foreign investment on their territories. In addition to the kinds of permission specified in section 19.07 and 19.08, *supra*, some governments may exercise such control, at least in part, through supervision of the process of incorporation;[11] thus, in organizing a corporation in some countries, the foreigner may be required to follow different procedures and to meet different requirements from those applicable to host country nationals. For example, local law may provide that no foreigner may organize a corporation without first obtaining the approval of the country's foreign investment agency.

While capital requirements in U.S. corporate statutes are minimal or non-existent, one often finds that incorporation in some countries requires a relatively high initial capitalization. For example, the formation of a *societe anonyme* in France requires an initial capital of 100,000 francs, while the German *Aktien Gesellshaft* necessitates a minimum stated and paid-in capital of 100,000 deutsche mark.

---

[11] R. M. Buxbaum, *The Formation of Marketable Share Companies* 5 (1974), in XIII *Business and Private Enterprises, International Encyclopedia of Comparative Law*.

Capital requirements for private companies, such as the S.A.R.L. and the G.m.b.H., are considerably less. As a practical matter, however, in the case of virtually all foreign investment projects, minimum capital requirements for incorporation are rarely so high as to constitute a significant obstacle.

In addition to the specific amounts of required capital, foreign company laws differ as to whether the initial capital must actually be paid in before the corporation may come into existence, or whether it must merely be subscribed to. For example, the Japanese law requires immediate payment of the entire subscription price of the stock, while the French and German laws permit installment payments.[12] Unlike American law, many foreign legal systems do not recognize the concept of authorized but unissued shares. Instead, they require that all authorized shares constituting the capital of the corporation be paid for, or at least subscribed to, at the time of formation. Under such a system, of course, any subsequent issuance of shares after incorporation will require, as a precondition, the amendment of the corporate charter to increase the authorized capital.

Many foreign company laws contain special provisions designed to protect the enterprise and its creditors in the event that the shares are to be paid for in property or in some other form of non-monetary consideration. For example, in an attempt to prevent the recipient from profiting from any possible over-evaluation of the property, French law prohibits the transfer of stock received for property for a fixed period of time. In addition, some countries require a special auditor or disinterested third party to value such property before the shares are issued.

Probably every legal system in the world requires the preparation and submission of documentation as part of the process of incorporation. Such documentation, which will normally include statutorily-required information—such as the corporate purpose, the names of the initial shareholders or incorporators, the amount of authorized capital, the address of the corporation, and other fundamental principles of its operation—is known by a variety of names, including "articles of incorporation," "corporate charter," "memorandum of association," or "statute." The complexity and extent of the documentation required for incorporation will vary from country to country. In some jurisdictions, the required information may be rudimentary

---

[12] Buxbaum, *supra* n.11, at 10–11.

§ 19.11[C]   INTERNATIONAL PLANNING   19–108

at best; in others, it may be extensive and include significant background data on the corporate promoters and initial shareholders. In addition to the statutory requirements, the organizers of the company may wish to include in the Articles other provisions and principles which are to govern the operation of the enterprise, particularly those provisions which the organizers do *not* want to be easily amended. Moreover, some countries, including the United Kingdom, may promulgate entire model articles or bylaws which all companies are to follow in preparing their own organizational documents. In addition to a basic document filed with the authorities, the company may also have a set of bylaws (sometimes referred to as Articles of Association, or *projet de statuts*) to govern matters of internal operation.[13]

A further legal requirement encountered in the process of incorporation involves the minimum number of incorporators and/or shareholders. Whereas the Model Business Corporation Act in the United States permits incorporation by one incorporator and recognizes the legality of the "one-person corporation" in which a single individual owns all the shares, many foreign legal systems reject either or both such possibilities. For example, the French *societe anonyme* requires a minimum of seven shareholders, while the German *Aktein Gesselschaft* mandates a minimum of five. Normally, with respect to private companies, such as the S.A.R.L. and G.m.b.H., the law requires a smaller minimum number of shareholders or incorporators than it does for public companies. Nonetheless, many civil law jurisdictions reject the idea of a one-person company, since they cling to the notion that a company is basically a contract requiring two or more persons. In such jurisdictions, if all the shares of the company fall into the hands of a single person, such occurrence may be grounds for dissolution of the enterprise or for holding the single shareholder liable for the debts of the company. These provisions covering the minimum number of shareholders and incorporators may require careful planning if the investor seeks to undertake a wholly-owned subsidiary.

After the drafting of the articles and other necessary documentation, the investor must ordinarily file them with an appropriate public institution. In many countries, particularly those following the civil law tradition, such authority is an office attached to the civil or commercial court which keeps the commercial registry.[14] In other

---

[13] Buxbaum, *supra* n.11, at 12.

[14] Buxbaum, *supra* n.11, at 19.

countries, the appropriate institution is an administrative agency attached to the executive branch of government. In addition to filing appropriate documents, the incorporators may be required to undertake some form of publicity, such as a legal announcement in a newspaper or a summary of the articles in the official gazette or special government publication for that purpose. Once registration and notice have been completed, the corporation comes into existence in most legal systems.[15]

The company laws of many countries may require a control structure which departs from that prevailing in the United States. Most American corporate codes generally vest responsibility for the management of the corporation in a Board of Directors elected by the shareholders. The Board of Directors selects officers to carry out the day-to-day activities, and such officers generally have no more authority than that which the Board delegates to them. Foreign company laws may provide for a model of control that is either more simple or more complex than in the United States. In some countries, management of a private company may be vested in a single "manager" (*gerant*) who has full powers to represent the company, thereby obviating the necessity of a board of directors. On the other hand, management structure for many foreign public companies–and even certain classes of private companies–can be more complex than that found in the United States. For example, many foreign legal systems provide for a "two-tiered" system of management which calls for (1) a Board of Management which has the responsibility for handling the day-to-day affairs, and a (2) Supervisory Board whose basic function is the election and removal of the Executive Board, the approval of financial accounts, and the general supervision of corporate activity. Thus the Supervisory Board's primary responsibility is to monitor the activities of management and to report to the shareholders.

The American businessperson and lawyer should be aware that many countries use their company laws to implement social and economic policies to a far greater degree than is common in the corporate codes of the United States. As a result, the investor seeking to organize an enterprise may find imbedded in foreign corporate laws various principles which reflect peculiar economic and social orientations and which may complicate the operation of the subsidiary. For

---

[15] Buxbaum, *supra* n.11, at 19–20.

example, the company laws of many countries require worker participation in both management and profit-sharing as an inherent part of the corporate structure. The nature and extent of such participation varies from country to country. With respect to management, the workers may actually hold seats on the Board of Directors, or they may be relegated to making recommendations which the Board of Directors is required to consider. Similarly, the company law may provide that a specific portion of each year's profits is to be allocated to the workers or to their organizations. Other social and economic objectives may be pursued through requirements on the qualifications to hold the position of manager or member of the Board. For example, some countries may require that only nationals be managers or hold board positions or a portion thereof. Others may impose minimum or maximum age requirements and stipulate that the manager or directors hold a minimum number of shares. Because of such provisions, the American lawyers may find that few foreign company laws grant the business person the freedom to organize a corporation to the same degree that such freedom exists in the United States.

§ 19.12 Other Host Country Laws Affecting Foreign Investment

Investment codes and companies legislation are not, of course, the only laws to have a direct effect upon the process of undertaking a foreign investment project. Indeed, the investor and his counsel must be aware that the investment project will have to operate within a complex web of foreign legislation and rules—many of which are unfamiliar—that can severely affect the profitability of the project. In the space available in this section, one can only cite a few of the more significant host country laws which the investor must carefully examine before undertaking an investment project.

Exchange control laws and regulations are among the most significant of such legislation in many countries. Section 2.04, *supra*, discusses the nature and structure of such laws, and the reader would be well advised to review that discussion. In countries where a pervasive system of exchange controls exist, the investor will often seek to obtain guarantees from the central bank or ministry of finance that specified amounts of foreign exchange will be available for needed purposes, such as the repatriation of profits, servicing of foreign debt, payment of foreign royalties, and the importation of components and raw materials. In countries that do not currently have an exchange control system, the investor may nonetheless face a major problem, in that after an investment project has been established, the government, for pressing financial reasons, may impose foreign exchange laws and regulations that will have a serious impact on the project and may curtail its profitability. Thus, in establishing a project, the investor not only has to examine existing foreign exchange laws and rules, but must also seek to make an educated prediction about the likelihood of the imposition of new controls in the future.[1] On the other hand, the existence of a bilateral investment treaty, as was discussed in section 19.04, supra, obligating the parties to give the right to make monetary transfers freely may serve to exempt investors from the subsequent imposition of an exchange control system.

Labor legislation is another area of concern. While prevailing hourly wages in many countries appear to be extremely low, existing labor legislation may impose additional costs on the project so as to make the real cost of labor significantly higher than originally supposed.

---

[1] The sudden imposition of exchange control legislation in Mexico in 1982 was a graphic example.

For example, the labor laws of many host countries make it virtually impossible for an enterprise to discharge a worker; consequently, in times of low demand, the project will be unable to reduce its payroll. Moreover, it may even be exceptionally difficult, except upon payment of a substantial indemnity, to discharge a worker who is inefficient or dishonest. In addition, the labor and social legislation of the host country may require the payment of substantial benefits for social security, medical insurance, vacation pay, and housing and clothing allowances. The existence of such laws may, of course, have a significant impact upon the choice of technology in a particular project and on the methods for selecting and hiring workers. Host country laws will also normally set down a framework for industrial relations. In many developing nations, for example, the law may forbid workers to strike, but instead require the parties to go through a form of arbitration and mediation.

Many countries impose a system of price controls on the sale of goods—particularly commodities which are in short supply. The possibility that such controls may apply to the output of the investment project will of course raise serious concern with respect to its long-term profitability. In countries where price controls exist, investors are often involved in a constant process of negotiation with the government to raise the applicable control level. On the other hand, the project may profit from price controls if they are applicable to raw materials and components and thereby assure a low cost of production.

Land law may also have a significant impact upon the project. In this area, not only will the investor encounter the written law concerning security of title or the validity of a lease, but he may also have to deal with unwritten rules which are customary in nature. The legal systems of many countries, particularly in the third world, recognize the validity of unwritten customary rights, which may be based on tribal law or some other law which is ethnic in origin. Consequently, even though the host country government may purport to grant the foreign investor a lease or even a freehold interest in land, such grant may be encumbered with the customary rights of local persons and groups, and the investor will have to undertake a process of negotiation and payment to extinguish the customary rights attaching to the land. For example, the holder of a concession for the development of a large agricultural scheme may be required to negotiate with, and pay compensation to, nomadic herdsmen who have traditionally grazed their cattle on the land in question. Similarly, in certain large urban areas, individuals may have established "squatters rights" on land which the investor is proposing to use for the project. In situations such as these, the investor may have to employ the services of an anthropologist or sociologist to determine the very existence of rights and the potential sources of conflict with respect to his land, despite claims from the host country government that the land has been granted "free and clear of all other rights."

§ 19.13 Debt-To-Equity Conversion: A New Approach to Investment in Developing Countries

[A] Background

In the wake of the dramatic oil price rises of the 1970s, many developing countries responded to severe balance of payments deficits by borrowing funds abroad from international commercial banks. Even countries with petroleum resources chose this approach because it offered a means of financing development at a quickened pace. As a result, the nations of the third world accumulated a substantial burden of debt, which by 1987 amounted to nearly $800 billion.[1]

These developing country loans were basically of two types:

1. Credits extended to private sector enterprises, and

2. "Sovereign debt," that is, loans to national governments, central banks, or state-owned enterprises, as well as private debt that had been assumed by governments as a result of a public guarantee. Sovereign debts constituted by far the largest portion of developing country obligations.

By 1982, it had become clear that many developing countries were unable to service their debts in a timely way and that the credit worthiness of their obligations was questionable. The developing countries were suffering from the combined effects of (1) rising debt service costs due to higher interest rates, (2) reduced commodity exports due to an economic recession in many parts of the world, and (3) increased payments abroad due to sharply higher oil prices. All of these factors provoked a debt crisis, which began in August 1982 when Mexico announced that it was unable to make payments on its $80 billion in foreign loans.

Since sovereign governments and state entities are not subject to bankruptcy or forced liquidation of assets, the inability of developing countries to make payments of principal and interest as they became due left the international commercial banks no alternative but to begin a process of 'rescheduling' debt payments—that is, of negotiating an extension of the period over which payments would be made. The major banks dominated this rescheduling process, and the smaller banks involved in the loan syndications felt obligated to participate.

---

[1] International Monetary Fund, World Economic Outlook 247 (1986). *See supra* § 2.03[D] (summary of debt crisis).

The effect of the failure of developing countries to make payments in a timely fashion, when coupled with the rescheduling process, raised the question of the value of the loans that the banks held in their portfolios, and this concern placed pressure on many banks to try to relieve or adjust their exposure in developing countries.

These factors led to the creation of a secondary market among the banks for developing country debt obligations. Banks began to trade or "swap" obligations on a discounted basis among themselves, an activity that became known as "debt swaps." The banks would trade debt among themselves for a variety of reasons. The smaller banks with limited exposure in a particular developing country might seek to eliminate that exposure completely by selling or swapping the debt. Large banks, on the other hand, might enter the "loan-swap market" to balance or adjust their portfolios. For example, a bank with significant Latin American debt might agree with another bank to exchange a portion of that debt for eastern European debt which the second bank was holding, in order to give its loan portfolio a more balanced geographic exposure.[2] Other banks, to reduce the administrative costs of rescheduling debt in numerous countries, used the debt-swap market to consolidate their third world exposure to a few countries, thereby allowing them to concentrate their rescheduling efforts. For whatever reason a bank might enter this market, such "swaps" were also advantageous because the pure barter of one debt obligation for another did not require the banks to recognize a loss for accounting purposes. This new secondary market in developing country debt gave banks greater flexibility in managing their portfolios than in the past, when their only option had been merely to hold the loan to maturity.

For the first few years, loan swaps were purely an interbank matter. Once in a while, however, a speculator might purchase a loan at a significant discount in hopes of making a profit if the loan were paid in full at maturity. In 1985, changes in the laws and policies of certain developing countries led to the creation of a new group of buyers who entered the secondary market in order to purchase loans at a discount and then convert them to equity investments in the developing country

---

[2] *See* Ollard, *The Debt Swappers,* Euromoney, Aug. 1986, at 67, 74-75 (swap of Nicaraguan for Venezuelan debt proved successful for bank); Newman, *LDC Debt: The Secondary Market, the Banks, and New Investment in the Developing Countries,* Colum. J. World Bus., Fall 1986, at 69, 69-70 (discussing portfolio management).

that owed the debt.[3] Chile was the first to act in this area. Beginning in 1985, it allowed persons holding Chilean external debt, which was selling at a significant discount, to exchange it for local currency at or near the face value of the obligation and to use the proceeds for certain specified investment purposes within Chile. Thus, through this process, debt was "swapped" or converted into equity investment in Chile itself. Over time, other countries, including Mexico, the Philippines, and Brazil, adopted similar laws and policies to permit debt-to-equity conversions, thereby creating a new mechanism for encouraging foreign investment in their territories. By the end of 1987, it was estimated that nearly $10 billion in developing country debt had been converted to equity investment through this process.[4] In addition to those countries which have established formal debt-to-equity conversion programs, others have engaged in this process on an ad hoc basis. The technique of debt-to-equity conversion appears to be attracting increasing attention throughout the developing world, and it is quite possible that many other nations may use it as a means to promote foreign investment. As a result, persons planning investments in developing countries should be aware of this option and understand its implications.

[B] The Types of Conversion Transactions

Debt conversions generally cover three types of transactions: debt capitalizations; debt-for-equity investments; and debt-for-local-currency conversions. All three are referred to commonly as "debt-swaps."

[1] Debt Capitalization Transactions

In debt capitalizations, the holder of a loan of a developing country obligor converts it into an equity interest in the same obligor, usually without an intervening transaction. The holder of the obligation might

---

[3] *See, e.g.,* World Bank, *Report on Chilean Debt Conversion,* Sept. 24, 1986, reprinted at 26 Int'l Legal Materials 819 (1987); *Philippines: Explanatory Memorandum on Philippine Investment Notes,* 26 Int'l Legal Materials 808 (1987); *Decree No. 1521,* Gaceta Oficial de la Republica de Venezuela, Apr. 14, 1987, at 1, translated at 26 Int'l Legal Materials 801 (1987); Schubert, *Trading Debt for Equity,* Banker, Feb. 1987, at 18, 20 (Mexican rules). *See generally Recent Development,* 28 Harv. Int'l L.J. 507 (1987) (discussing programs in Chile, Mexico, and the Philippines). For an example of an agreement covering the assignment of Chilean debt, see Appendix 19C, *infra.*

[4] Wall St. J., Aug. 13, 1987, at 3, col. 2.

be either the original lender to the enterprise or a person who has acquired the obligation, usually at a significant discount, in the secondary market. The impetus for the transaction is often the inability of the enterprise to make payment on its loan. Generally, debt capitalization is not applicable in the case of sovereign debt. Many developing country investment laws contain provisions which permit or encourage the conversion of a loan to an enterprise into an equity investment in the same enterprise.

[2] Debt-for-Equity Transactions

The laws of some countries now provide a mechanism whereby the investor may convert the debt of one obligor into an equity investment in a totally different entity. Such debt-for-equity conversion is normally carried out in a series of steps. First, the investor wishing to make an investment in a particular developing country purchases the debt obligations of that country at a significant discount in the secondary market. Second, the authorities in that country agree to convert the obligation at or near its face value in local currency if the investor agrees to invest such proceeds in a project approved by the host country authorities. Third, the host country government or the central bank provides the investor local currency or its equivalent, and the investor proceeds to make the investment under conditions stipulated by the host country authorities. It is this type of transaction, aimed at stimulating new investment by foreigners, that has been the subject of greatest attention by developing countries.

[3] Debt-for-Local Currency Transactions

In order to attract the foreign currency holdings of their own nationals, some developing countries have facilitated the purchase of foreign debt by their nationals and its subsequent conversion into local currency at or near face value. Their nationals may then use the local currency in their home country, but not necessarily for investment alone. Debt for local currency conversion is basically a mechanism to facilitate the repatriation of capital that was previously taken out of the country by its own citizens.

[C] Reasons for the Development of Debt-Equity Conversions

As can be seen, no debt-equity conversion transaction can take place without the approval—indeed the active encouragement—of the host country government. The conversion of a foreign obligation selling at a large discount abroad into local currency at the obligation's face value requires the cooperation of the Central Bank, Ministry of Finance, and national monetary authorities. Further, the investment of those funds will necessitate the approval of the agencies responsible for regulating foreign investment.

Certain countries have chosen to adopt laws and obligations to facilitate this process. A variety of reasons have prompted this action. First, the debt-for-equity conversion process is viewed as a means for reducing—albeit in a limited way—the country's foreign debt and therefore its payments of foreign exchange for debt servicing.[5] Second, to the extent that debt-equity conversion leads to new foreign investment, the country will benefit from increased productive capacity, employment, technology transfers, tax revenues, and economic activity. In those countries whose political climate may not permit changes in existing foreign investment laws and policies, a debt-for-equity conversion program may allow a government to encourage foreign investment indirectly when it could not do so directly. Similarly, it may also be a politically acceptable way of re-attracting capital that its own nationals have previously taken from he country by questionable means.[6]

For the foreign investor, debt-to-equity conversion offers an opportunity to make an investment more cheaply than would be possible by a direct infusion of foreign currency which would be converted at the official rate of exchange. In effect, the host country is subsidizing such investment by allowing the foreign investor, through the use of external debt purchased at a discount, to obtain local currency at a highly advantageous exchange rate. For example, if the foreign investor is able to buy host country foreign debt in the secondary market at a 50-percent discount and then to convert it to local currency at face value, the host government is, in effect, giving the investor a special exchange rate that will bring him twice the amount of local currency he would have received had he merely undertaken an investment by a direct infusion of foreign funds. In order to relate the size of the subsidy to the magnitude of the benefit to be derived from the investor, Mexico redeems its debt at varying percentages of the face value, depending on the importance of the investment to be

---

[5] *See A Lesson from Chile,* Economist, Mar. 7, 1987, at 87.

[6] *See* Schubert, *supra* n.3, at 18-19.

undertaken. In addition to the problem of subsidizing investments unnecessarily, debt-equity conversions are criticized on the grounds that through this approach developing countries are needlessly prepaying their debts to the international banks.

For international commercial banks, debt-for-equity conversion offers a means of reducing developing country exposure, since the purchase of the debt by an investor removes it from a bank's portfolio. Moreover, it allows banks to earn fees for arranging or brokering debt-equity transactions.[7]

All of these factors have given significant impetus to the debt-for-equity approach to investment in some developing countries. Most countries, however, have resisted the trend thus far, for they have been concerned about certain difficulties.[8] First, they fear that this approach in many cases merely gives an unnecessary subsidy to foreign investment that would have taken place in any event without a debt-for-equity program. Thus, many developing country governments seek assurance that the debt-equity approach will bring them new investment that they would not otherwise have obtained.

Second, host countries fear that this mechanism will in the end merely facilitate the outflow of capital through eventual repatriation of the investment and through the payment of fees and dividends abroad. To deal with this problem, countries that have adopted the debt-equity approach often impose conditions on how the local currency, once converted, may be used. Chile, for example, provides that the capital from investments made through this mechanism may not be repatriated abroad for a period of ten years and that profits must accumulate during the first four years after the investment is made and may be repatriated only thereafter.

A further concern is that the increase in local currency pumped into the economy to extinguish the foreign debt may have serious inflationary effects within the host country. In some cases, instead of issuing currency, the host government may choose to issue obligations; but this method may have the effect of enlarging national budgetary deficits.[9] In formulating their laws and regulations on debt-equity

---

[7] *See generally* Bentley, *Debt Conversion in Latin America*, Colum. J. World Bus., Fall 1986, at 37, 38-39 (discussing advantages to creditors).

[8] *See generally* Recent Development, 28 Harv. Int'l L.J. 507, 513 (1987).

[9] *See* Fierman, *Fast Bucks in Loan Swaps*, Fortune, Aug. 3, 1987, at 92, 96; Moreno, *LDC Debt Swaps*, Fed. Reserve Bank of San Francisco Weekly Letter, Sept. 4, 1987, at 2-3 (discussing arbitrage possibilities).

conversion programs, developing countries have tried to blunt the potential inflationary and negative budgetary consequences. One approach is to limit the amount to be converted. Chile, for example, determines the total amount it will convert each month and then allocates this quota by holding an auction of conversion rights among interested persons.[10]

Beyond the direct impact of this debt-equity conversion on the local economy is the question of its effect on the third world's relationships with the international banks. On the one hand, it may be argued that this process allows banks to lessen their exposure (albeit at a cost) in a given country while rehabilitating the credit of that country in the international economic community. On the other hand, by reducing pressure on the banks, debt-equity swaps weaken the ability of the developing countries to attain their fundamental objective—outright debt relief. It is still too early to determine the precise consequences of this innovation, which links two previously separate issues: third world debt and foreign investment in developing countries.

[D] The Structure of Debt-Equity Transactions

The laws and regulations governing debt-for-equity conversions are generally complex and vary significantly from country to country. Structuring a debt-to-equity transaction requires careful attention to the relevant legislation, as well as to the underlying loan agreement. With regard to the latter, it is important to structure the transaction so that it does not violate the *pari passu* clauses in most loan agreements prohibiting the payment of one creditor in preference to another. Rescheduling agreements between developing countries and their principal bank creditors typically contain provisions permitting debt-equity conversion provided that the investor's rights of repatriation are limited, at least for a period of time.

To illustrate the nature of such a transaction, the following is a step-by-step example of structuring a debt-to-equity under the Chilean program in accordance with Chapter XIX of Chile's Central Bank regulations. As described in a World Bank report,[11] these are the steps that a foreign investor—in most instances a multinational corporation—would have to undertake to accomplish a direct investment through a debt-equity swap.

---

[10] *See Recent Development, supra* n.8, at 508-9.

[11] World Bank, *Report on Chilean Debt Conversion, supra* n.3, at 834-36.

1. The foreign investor, wishing to make an investment in Chile, contacts a foreign broker dealing in LDC debt in order to locate a Chilean foreign debt instrument available for prepayment at a discount. The foreign investor will have to use foreign exchange to purchase the debt and will have to pay the broker a fee for completing the transaction.

2. Once the foreign broker has found an appropriate debt instrument, the foreign investor obtains the agreement of the Chilean debtor to redenominate the debt at its face value into local currency at the official exchange rate.

3. The foreign investor then applies to the Central Bank to obtain permission to make an investment in Chile with the local currency proceeds of the debt capitalization transaction. The application must describe the project in detail and identify all parties involved. The investor must also accept restrictions on its ability to repatriate capital and profits. Moreover, the Central Bank may require the investor to waive the free repatriation provisions applicable to its prior investments and even to make a portion of the new investment in foreign exchange, in addition to the proceeds of the debt-equity swap.

4. Having obtained the necessary authorizations, the foreign investor actually purchases the debt instrument at a discount through its broker and pays the broker's fee. Normally, a debt rescheduling agreement between the country's creditor banks and its central Bank will have authorized the assignment of such debt.[12]

5. The investor delivers the note to a Chilean bank along with an irrevocable mandate to collect in cash the face value of the redenominated note or to exchange it for a new instrument payable in local currency.

6. The Chilean bank, with the prior approval of the foreign creditor bank and the Chilean debtor, redenominates the debt in local currency equal to the face value of the foreign obligation converted at the official exchange rate, thus transforming the foreign exchange obligation.

7. The Chilean bank creates a new local currency debt instrument with the Chilean debtor as the direct obligor payable to bearer and denominated in Chilean currency and payable, for example, over 15

---

[12] *See* Appendix 19C, *infra*, for an example of an agreement assigning Chilean debt.

years. The foreign debt instrument (now denominated in local currency) is canceled and the new instrument is delivered to the Chilean broker.

8. The Chilean broker places the debt instrument in the domestic financial market and delivers the local currency proceeds to the Chilean bank with a mandate to disburse the funds directly for the purchase of the approved equity shares or other form of investment.

9. The equity shares or other evidence of the investment are delivered to the foreign investor.

§ 19.14 Privatization of Government Assets: Another Mechanism for Foreign Investment

[A] Background

As the decade of the 1980s drew to a close, countries in all corners of the world and at every level of development were seeking with increasing speed to introduce the market forces of capitalism into their economies. This trend has been known generally as "privatization." A specific form of privatization has been the sale or transfer of public assets or interests therein to private investors.[1] These public assets have included state-owned enterprises operating in virtually every economic sector, from agriculture and manufacturing to transportation and communications. Governments in countries that were once eager to establish national airlines and government steel mills are now just as eager to sell those same airlines and steel mills to private investors, both domestic and foreign.

The phenomenon of privatization began principally in developed countries in the early 1980s, especially when the British government privatized British TeleCom through the sale to the public of $4.9 billion worth of its shares. Among developing countries, Chile, an early leader, began the process of selling its state-owned enterprises in 1974.[2] The trend developed with increased force in both developed and developing countries. Worldwide receipts from the sale of state assets exceeded $25 billion in both 1989 and 1990, and reached nearly $50 billion in 1991. Between 1984 and 1991, total receipts from privatization transactions amounted to approximately $250 billion.[3] Observers expect divesting countries throughout the world to realize an equivalent amount during the decade of the 1990's.

Countries as different in political structure and social system as Mongolia, the United Kingdom, Tunisia, Mexico, and Malaysia have adopted privatization programs; however, their individual reasons for doing so have varied from country to country. Many experts and policy makers believe that privatization is crucial to economic liberalization and reform, both in industrialized countries and in the Third World.

---

[1] R. Hemming, & Ali M. Munsoor, Privatization and Public Enterprises 1 (International Monetary Fund, Occasional Paper 56, January 1988).

[2] H.B. Nankani, *Lessons of Privatization in Developing Countries*, 27 Fin. & Dev. 43 (March 1990). Between 1974 and 1990, Chile privatized approximately 400 state-owned enterprises.

[3] *Escaping the Heavy Hand of the State*, Economist, 73 (June 13, 1992).

The existence of privatization programs in so many countries has created new opportunities for foreign investors. Indeed, foreign investors have provided much capital to the process of privatization since the trend began. Rather than establish new enterprises, many foreign investors have chosen to purchase existing state-owned enterprises or their assets, reorganize them, and then attempt to operate them on a profitable basis. In many countries lacking sufficient local capital, technology and management skills, the governments concerned aim their privatization program primarily to foreign investors and multinational corporations who have those crucial resources. As a result, in many parts of the world, countries that were once reluctant to admit foreign capital and that placed severe restrictions on direct foreign investment, have through their new privatization laws and programs now created incentives and opportunities for direct foreign investment in their countries.

In addition to direct foreign investment, privatization programs present multinational companies with two other types of business opportunities. First, certain types of privatization creates possibilities of foreign portfolio investment by individuals, firms and institutional investors located abroad. Some countries have chosen to make international public offerings of shares in their formerly state-owned enterprises, thereby enabling investors in many countries to obtain equity interests in those enterprises. In effect, international stock offering tied to privatization programs in particular countries, such as Malaysia and Singapore, are contributing to the integration of global equity markets.

A third type of business opportunity relates to the services that multinational firms can provide to governments and their state enterprises in executing the privatization process itself. In order to privatize successfully, many governments have had to seek the help of foreign investment bankers, law firms, accounting firms, and other types of consulting organizations, to plan privatization programs and to carry out the various transactions needed to complete those programs successfully. These services include the identification and reorganization of enterprises appropriate for privatization, valuation of those enterprises, preparation of offering circulares, introduction of new, internationally recognized accounting systems, financial restructuring, and negotiating and drafting the contracts which will execute the individual privatization transaction.

In addition to creating opportunities for multinational companies and other foreign investors, privatization may also present them with new challenges. For example, a formerly uncompetitive state enterprises, as a result of the introduction of new capital, management and technology, may become new and aggressive competitors in the international market. Moreover, a multinational company's existing competitors may use the privatization process to gain a foot hold or a dominant position in a given country's market by buying a formerly stated-owned enterprise.

For these reasons, it is important for multinational companies and their attorneys to understand the privatization process and its effect on undertaking foreign investments. This section will examine the reasons why governments have decided to privatize and the techniques they employ in carrying out privatization. It will also discuss of the related legal problems.

[B] Reasons and Objectives for Privatization Programs

Governments have launched privatization programs for a variety of reasons.[4] The countries of Eastern and Central Europe have undertaken privatization in an attempt to dismantle state controlled, Communist economies that failed to give a satisfactory life to their people. Other countries have embarked on privatization to raise much needed government revenues. Over 90 governments have undertaken privatization programs of some sort in recent years.[5] In doing so they have pursued a variety of objectives, depending on the particular situation of the country concerned. These varied objectives have in turn shaped the nature of the privatization process, defined the opportunities offered to foreign investors, and determined the mechanisms used to transfer public assets into private hands. As a result, it is important for the attorney who advises clients contemplating foreign investment through a privatization program in a particular country to understand clearly the objectives pursued by the government concerned.

Such governmental objectives include the following or some combination thereof:

1. Relief of High Governmental Budget Deficits

---

[4] For a comprehensive discussion of privatization see Charles Vuylsteke, Techniques of Privatization of State-Owned Enterprises, Volume I Methods and Implementation. (World Bank Technical Paper Number 88, 1988). See also R. Ramamurti, *Why Are Developing Countries Privatizing?* 23 J. Int'l Bus. Stud. 225 (1992).

[5] Nankani, *supra* n.2 at 44.

The 1960s and the 1970s witnessed a great expansion in state-owned enterprises, particularly in developing countries.[6] For the most part, these state-owned enterprises proved inefficient and unprofitable. Governments were only able to maintain them by providing subsidies from the state budget. Such subsidies, when combined with other adverse economic circumstances, led to increasing budgetary deficits for those governments. Also, many governments found that the management of state owned enterprises placed a heavy administrative burden on the government itself. To obtain relief from these burdens and to reduce budget deficits, many governments have decided to sell inefficient state owned enterprises to private investors, both foreign and domestic.

2. Relief from High Foreign Indebtedness

Many governments financed the development of their public sector enterprises through heavy foreign borrowing. As a result of the debt crisis of the 1980s, these same governments found themselves unable to service these debts. In order to reduce the debt burden, many governments decided to sell off the indebted private enterprises.

3. Improvement of the Efficiency of State-Owned Enterprises

Many of the state owned enterprises were inefficient and poorly managed. Protected by subsidies, high tariffs, and government regulations, they often had no incentive to develop efficient, profitable operations. Governments also used state-owned enterprises to absorb unemployment; consequently, they often had too many workers to operate at a profit. In order to improve the efficiency of state owned enterprises, many governments privatized them in order to place them under effective private management and to subject them to the competitive discipline of market economic forces.

4. To Increase Competition

Many state-owned enterprises had a virtual monopoly over specific products or economic sectors in the countries concerned. Inevitably, such monopolies produced goods and services of low quality and high prices. In the 1980s, governments became convinced of the benefits of economic competition as a way to improve the quality of goods and services, to make operations more efficient, and to lower prices.

---

[6] In Chile, for example, the number of public enterprises grew from 46 in 1970 to 600 by the end of 1973. Nankani, *supra* n.2 at 43.

These governments embarked on policies of breaking up large state-owned enterprises and selling them off in small groups in order to foster a competitive environment in particular economic sectors or the economy as a whole.

5. To Foster the Development of Productive Private Enterprises

Many governments, convinced of the value of an active private sector, undertook privatization programs in order to improve business conditions by fostering the development of private enterprises. In the face of large state-owned enterprises that were dominating specific economic sectors, private entrepreneurs found it very difficult to enter the market. Privatization was the means to encourage the growth of private enterprise.

6. Development of Wider Business Ownership

Many governments also wanted to bring about a wider public ownership of business and to mobilize public savings for economic development purposes through distribution of ownership interests in their state-owned enterprises. The fostering of stock markets and public equity markets necessitated wide ownership by the public of business enterprises, a goal that was pursued through the privatization of states-owned enterprises.

7. Implementation of Pre-existing Policies

Many governments established state-owned enterprises or purchased failing private companies with a declared purpose of only launching a national industry or playing a catalytic role in the economy. In short, their stated purpose at the time was not to make the government the permanent owner or manager of business enterprises, but rather just to get them underway. Some governments have evoked these policies to justify privatization programs of state enterprises that were purchased or created at an earlier time.

8. To Satisfy the Demands of International Financial Institutions

International financial institutions such as The World Bank and the International Monetary Fund have encouraged the privatization process. Indeed, they have often conditioned their assistance on government commitment to undertake a privatization program. These international agencies have favored privatization since they felt that the state owned enterprises had resulted in big budget deficits, large external indebtedness, all of which would prevent governments from attaining fiscal soundness. In order to obtain needed financial assistance from these international agencies, the governments have been led to adopt privatization programs.

Often, the decision in a particular country to undertake privatization has been prompted by a combination of two or more of the objectives stated above. For example, Tunisia, which has had what is considered by many the most successful privatization program in Africa, sought both to open up its market to international competition and to attract more foreign investment into the country. Mongolia, like the economies of Eastern and Central Europe, has used privatization as a tool to move from a centrally planned economy to a market economy. The preamble to Senegal's 1987 law on privatization lists four main objectives: autonomy and accountability of enterprise management; mobilization of public and private savings into productive investments; reduction of subsidies to state owned enterprises; and encouragement of widespread share ownership.[7]

[C] The Legal Basis of Privatization

In considering a privatization transaction, an attorney should first seek to determine the legal basis for the privatization program in the country concerned. Privatization is the transfer of public assets into private hands, a serious matter in any nation. It is therefore important to ascertain the legal authority for making such a transfer. Such legal authorization may take many forms, depending on the country's constitutional and legal structure.

The constitution itself may require amendment of provisions that prevent or impede privatization. For example, a constitution may state that state-owned enterprises may not be transferred to private interests or that certain sectors, such as petroleum or energy, which the government now wants to privatize, may only be exploited by the state.[8]

Even if the constitution does not prohibit privatization, many countries require an act of the legislature to authorize privatization, either because:

1) the constitution, as in many French-speaking African countries, requires a law to transfer assets from the public domain to the private sector or

---

[7] Vuylsteke, *supra* n.4 at 58.

[8] William B. Berenson, *Legal Considerations and the Role of Lawyers in the Privatization Process: An Overview,* 37 Fed. B. News & J. 159, 160 (March/April 1990).

2) the state-owned enterprise itself was created by a legislative act and therefore only a similar type of act can legally authorize its privatization.

Moreover, in many countries privatization represents such a departure from the existing situation, that a law is necessary to establish a permanent structure for the privatization process, to assure investors of the security of rights obtained in privatized property, to give clear authority to specific agencies to enter into privatization transactions, and to prevent courts and administrative agencies from subsequently canceling rights granted to investors. On the other hand, there are certain cases where no specific privatization law is necessary because the relevant administrative agency or executive department already has full legal power to dispose of state assets under its control. This is often the case with government holding companies, such as Italy's Instituto per la Ricostruzione Industriale (IRI), who want to sell their subsidiaries.

The legislative act authorizing privatization may either;

1) establish a general framework law for the sale of all state-owned enterprises or

2) designate a particular group or class of state-owned enterprises, either by specific reference to identified companies or to companies in particular economic sectors.

Poland adopted the first approach in its law on privatization of state-owned enterprises,[9] but France's law authorized the privatization of sixty-five specified state-owned organizations.[10] In a few countries, however, such as the United Kingdom, a third approach is found: a law is enacted for each state enterprise that is privatized.

In addition to authorizing privatization, these laws also specify the agency that is to carry out the privatization program, the procedures to be followed, and the conditions and terms that are applicable to privatization transactions. Some countries have created a new department or ministry to implement the privatization program; others have entrusted this responsibility to an existing governmental department. In either case, it is important for the foreign investor to determine

---

[9] Law on Privatization of State-Owned Enterprises of July 13, 1990, 29 Int'l Legal Materials 1226 (1990).

[10] Id.

precisely the extent of the department's authority to engage in privatization transactions.

The transfer of public assets into private hands obviously has risks of abuse. One of the principal purposes of privatization procedures and guidelines is to protect the public interest, including securing a fair price to the state and assuring that the purchaser is capable of operating the enterprise productively. The law may also specify the interest or link, if any, that the state must maintain or preserve in the privatized enterprise. It should be noted, however, that foreigners may not necessarily be given unfettered opportunities to participate in a privatization program. Some countries, continuing to be concerned about foreign domination of their economies, may retain restrictions on foreign investment even though they seek to privatize many public enterprises. Other countries, recognizing that their nationals do not have sufficient capital to purchase privatized enterprises or sufficient expertise to run them, do not restrict the participation of foreigners in privatization programs.

On the other hand, whether the purchaser is local or foreign, most governments continue to be concerned about the operation of the enterprise after the sale. In this respect, the government in a privatization sale is unlike the ordinary private party who sells a business. The reasons for this continued governmental concern are numerous, including the privatized enterprise's impact on the national economy and the resulting condition of its workers. The government may manifest its concern by seeking in some way to influence or control the privatized company after the sale. In addition to using its regulatory power, a government may seek to influence a privatized enterprise by retaining some interest in it. For example, the government, after privatization, might continue to hold a majority interest, a minority interest, a special class of shares with increased voting rights, or a "special share" (sometimes called a "golden share"), which, while giving the government no right to participate in capital or profits, does enable it to send representatives to shareholder meetings, to veto certain important decisions, and even to appoint a number of directors.

In addition to the issue of the authority to privatize is the equally important question of the nature of the property rights that are transferred to the investor by virtue of the privatization process. The problem is particularly important in countries, such as those of the former Soviet Union and Eastern Europe which existed under Communist systems that did not recognize the right of private property and whose public enterprises did not "own" assets, land and natural resources in the same sense as that term is used in western legal systems. Often the nature of their public enterprises' rights in such assets were merely a leasehold or a right of management. Consequently, foreign investors participating in privatization need to ascertain with care the precise nature of the rights in the assets they are acquiring through the privatization process. Moreover, since those assets were obtained by the former communist governments through expropriation of private interests, foreign investors also need to determine the nature of their exposure to possible restitution claims by the former private owners.

[D] **The Process of Privatization**

The precise way in which government assets are privatized will depend on numerous factors, including the goals pursued by the government, the financial and physical condition of the state-owned enterprise, the nature of the local economy and capital markets, and the country's existing relationships with foreign lenders, multinational corporations and international aid agencies. In simplified terms, there are basically eight types of privatization transactions:

1) public offering of shares;
2) private sale of shares;
3) new private investment in a state-owned enterprise;
4) sale of assets belonging to a state-owned enterprise;
5) reorganization or break-up of state-owned enterprise;
6) a purchase by the management or employees of the state-owned enterprise itself;
7) a lease of state-owned assets; and
8) a management contract with private interests to manage state-owned enterprises or government assets.[11]

Before undertaking any of these transactions, a government must usually take a series of steps to prepare the enterprise for the privatization. Often the legislation authorizing the privatization program will specify the necessary preliminary measures, as well as the procedures to be followed in actually carrying out he privatization transaction. First, the government must determine what existing legal

---

[11] Section 19.12[E], *infra*, will examine each type of transaction.

requirements must be satisfied to privatize the enterprise. For example, the enterprise may have existing loan agreements and guarantee agreements with commercial banks and international aid agencies, which prohibit the government from selling its interest in or giving up its control over a state-owned enterprise. As a result, before it can privatize the enterprise, the government may have to pay off creditors, negotiate a release or in some way involve them in the privatization transaction. Even if no such provision exists in loan agreements, the fact that a creditor holds a mortgage, lien or other security interest in the assets of the enterprise may prevent the transfer of assets to private parties without the creditor's approval. It should be noted that governments often guarantee loans to state-owned enterprises by banks and international lending agencies. This fact raises the question of the continuing force of that guarantee if the enterprise is privatized. In most cases, the guarantee will continue after privatization unless the creditor agrees otherwise. As a result, the government is placed in the difficult position of guaranteeing the debts of an enterprise over which it no longer has control.

Another important set of legal considerations involve the internal organization of the state-enterprise that is to be privatized. For one thing, the legal form of a state enterprise may have to be converted into a private company. This may require the formation of a company under private law and the transfer of all the assets of the state enterprise to the newly created entity. For example, the Polish law on privatization provides for a two-stage privatization process. In the first stage, state-owned enterprises are legally transformed into private law corporations whose shares are wholly owned by the Polish State Treasury. In the second stage, the shares are sold to private investors, foreign or domestic, and the enterprise thus becomes privatized. Even if this step is not required, the articles of association or other fundamental document of enterprise will probably need amendment before privatization can take place.

A third set of legal changes relate to the general legal and regulatory framework within which the state-owned enterprise had operated. For example, if the law provided that only state-owned enterprises could operate in certain economic sectors, that legislation would have to be amended if the government hopes to privatize successfully enterprises operating in those sectors. Similarly price controls, credit regulations, and tax laws may need to be changed in order to create a business climate that is appropriate to private enterprise.

Other actions which a government needs to take before privatizing an enterprise include recapitalization, valuation of the enterprise, the introduction of realistic accounting methods, elimination of debt, and write-down of assets. Having done these things, the government then has a wide variety of techniques to choose form in structuring the privatization transaction.

[E] Types of Privatization Transactions

[1] Public Offering

One important method of privatizing a public enterprise is to sell all or a portion of its shares to the general public through a public offering. The mechanics of the transaction may be similar to an initial public offering of shares in a company in a western market economy, and would involve investment bankers, the preparation of a prospectus offering circular, and a stock distribution network. For a public offering to be successful, the following conditions have to be present:

1) the enterprise must be of substantial size with a reasonable earnings record and potential;

2) complete information on the firm must be prepared and made available to the investing public;

3) a local capital market of sufficient size and liquidity must exist;

4) mechanisms and institutions must exist to inform and attract the investing public.

Such conditions, however, exist in only a few developing countries. The main advantages of a public offering is that it allows widespread shareholding, is able to target the broad savings of the investing public, and is usually characterized by transparency and openness.

In some countries, such as Poland and the Czech Republic, governments have sought to achieve mass ownership of shares through the distribution to the public of vouchers or other certificates or book entry subscription rights for their citizens to use in acquiring shares in privatized enterprises. Often these rights are acquired for a relatively low sum. The voucher schemes have been criticized on the grounds that they fail to attract significant amounts of fresh capital either to the state treasury or to public enterprises. On the other hand, they do give a broad segment of the public a vested interest in privatization and the country's emerging market economy.

[2] Private Sale of Shares

In many countries and for many enterprises, a public offering of shares is not feasible. In such circumstances, the government concerned may decide to sell all or part of its shares in a state enterprise to a purchaser or group of purchasers through a privately negotiated transaction. Most privatization programs in developing countries have been done through a private sale of shares, rather than a public offering.

Often, the privatization law will specify how such transactions may be effected. Generally, they provide either for a competitive bidding process with publicity or for direct negotiation with identified potential purchasers. Such private sales do not have the openness and transparency of public offerings and may therefore be subject to abuse. As a result, the privatization law may specify special procedures to assure the government a fair price for the sale. The law will therefore state the methods of valuation, the procedures for competitive bidding, the criteria for selecting the winning bidders, and the process of negotiation to be conducted thereafter. Because the government's goal in most cases is to form a privatized company that continues to operate, the contract of sale may include conditions on the enterprise's continuing operations, as well as prohibitions against dismantling and selling its assets after privatization.

[3] Sale of Government or State Enterprise Assets

Rather than sell the whole enterprise, the government may decide to sell only some of its assets. The sale of assets can be based on open competitive bidding, an auction, or negotiation with an interested investor. For example, a state-owned airline may seek to focus exclusively on its core business and therefore sell off ancillary businesses, such as hotels, to private investors. Unlike the sale of shares in a going concern, an enterprise's assets are often sold without the related liabilities.

[4] Reorganization into Component Parts

Rather than merely sell assets, the state enterprise may divide itself into several component parts, incorporate them in the form of separate companies, and then sell them either by public offering or private sale of shares. This method permits privatization of an enterprise to take place at different times and under different conditions, to be determined by the government.

[5] New Private Investment in a State-Owned Enterprise

Rather than sell a state enterprise to private interests, the government may instead seek to introduce private capital into the existing enterprise, usually for purposes of modernization and expansion. In this type of transaction, the government is not selling its interest in the state-owned enterprise. Instead, its equity (and usually its control) is being diluted. The resulting enterprise is a "mixed" public-private company or joint venture. The continued presence of the government raises issues about the control structure so that the private investor can be assured that the enterprise will be managed in an efficient way that will maximize profits.[12]

[6] Management and/or Employee Buy-out

Often, the managers and/or employees of a state-owned enterprise are the most appropriate or, indeed, the only potential buyers of the enterprise or its assets. In this instance, the privatization of enterprise is effected by selling its assets or a controlling interest to a group of its managers and/or employees. This type of transaction usually requires external financing, which is then secured by the assets of the enterprise itself. Normally, the managers or workers first form a private company and then the shares or assets of the state enterprise are transferred to that company. Usually, this technique is used where the enterprise or its assets are not of interest to other investors. This type of transaction allows the government to avoid, at least temporarily, liquidations and the resulting employee lay-offs and dislocations.

[7] Leases

Instead of selling the assets or shares of a state enterprise to private investors, a government may privatize an enterprise by leasing its assets to private operators for a specified period in return for a fixed fee or rental. Although no transfer of ownership takes place in these transactions, the assets are placed under private management, which hopefully will operate them with increased efficiency and profitability. For example, a government which was unable to operate a state-owned steel mill profitably, leased it to a foreign investor for a fee, and the investor thereafter had the commercial risk of running it on a profitable basis. Sometimes such leases also give the lessee the option to purchase the assets under specified conditions.

---

[12] For a discussion of the issues related to joint ventures, see § 19.09 and § 19.10, *supra*.

[8] Management Contracts

Under a management contract, a private manager agrees to manage the state enterprise or assets in return for a fee. Under a management contract, unlike a lease, the state retains the commercial risk of the enterprise's operations. If the managed enterprise sustains a loss, the state must bear it.[13] The individual terms of leases and management contracts may blur the traditional distinction between these types of arrangements. For example, a manager's fee may be tied to the profitability of the enterprise and a lessee may be required to make an equity investment in the enterprise whose assets he has leased.

---

[13] For a discussion of management contracts, see § 12.08 *supra*.

§ 19.15 Foreign Investment in Infrastructure: Build-Operate-Transfer (BOT) and Build-Operate-Own (BOO) Arrangements.

[A] Background

Until the late 1980's, many countries did not permit direct foreign investment to play any role in infrastructure development. For strategic, nationalistic, and ideological reasons, their governments strongly believed that providing roads, ports, power, water, communications and other vital infrastructure services should not be done by foreigners but should be carried out only by national governmental entities. Governments, particularly in developing countries, feared that foreign control of infrastructure would lead to foreign domination of their economies and would ultimately impede their economic development and independence.

Since the late 1980's, however, this traditional resistance to foreign private infrastructure development has changed dramatically as more and more countries have adopted laws, regulations, and policies to allow foreign private investors to undertake all sorts of infrastructure projects, from roads and power plants to telecommunication systems and bridges. The reasons for this dramatic change are largely the same as the reasons, discussed in the preceding section, that caused governments to privatize their public sector industries. Large governmental fiscal deficits, heavy foreign indebtedness, inefficient government agencies and the need for massive amounts of capital to undertake large infrastructure projects vital to national economic development have made public financing of infrastructure projects difficult, and in some cases impossible, to meet the rising demand for infrastructure services. These factors have led governments to turn to the private sector—particularly the foreign private investors—for help in the construction, maintenance and operation of infrastructure projects that traditionally had been the sole responsibility of the government.

In recent years, significant changes in host country laws and policies have created new opportunities for foreign investors in infrastructure through Build-Operate-Transfer (BOT) and Build-Operate-Own (BOO) arrangements. The purpose of this section is to examine these innovative and important new foreign investment vehicles. Host countries employ the Build-Operate-Transfer (BOT) model of project financing for new construction projects in which a sponsoring foreign investor or consortium of investors and lenders supervises the construction and operation of an infrastructure facility, such as a road or power plant, for a determined length of time, and subsequently transfers ownership and control of the facility to the host government. Under the Build-Operate-Own (BOO) method, on the other hand, a sponsor or sponsoring consortium constructs and owns the infrastructure project, without a subsequent transfer of project assets to a host government. Both models, used primarily within the telecommunications, transportation and power generation industries, are in effect privatization techniques, and have become increasingly popular in developing countries as a method of infrastructure project financing.[1]

The basic distinction between the BOT and BOO models is the possibility in the former of future ownership by the state of the project. Eventual state ownership of the infrastructure facility may be important if the host government for ideological or political reasons believes it necessary to control sensitive economic activities that have strategic significance. In such cases, a host country will require a reversion of ownership to the government and therefore opt for a BOT model, rather than a BOO model, of project financing.[2] With this difference between the BOT and BOO model in mind, this section will refer only to the BOT arrangement. Other variations on the BOT and BOO models include: Build-Transfer (BT); Build, Lease and Transfer (BLT); Build, Transfer and Operate (BTO); Contract, Add and Operate (CAO); Develop, Operate and Transfer (DOT); Rehabilitate, Operate and Transfer (ROT); and Rehabilitate, Own and Operate (ROO). A BOT arrangement is a form of project finance. Project finance is a type of lending in which the lender relies on the assets and revenues of the project, rather than on the credit of the project sponsor, for repayment of loans. Loans in project financings are on a "nonrecourse" basis, which means that project sponsors and investors have no liability to lenders for repayment of project loans. For host governments, this factor is also an important advantage since the BOT form of project finance, unlike infrastructure financings in the past, has no impact on the country's level of outstanding indebtedness. At the heart of the

---

[1] Christopher J. Sozzi, *Comment: Project Finance and Facilitating Telecommunications Infrastructure Development in Newly-Industrializing Countries*, 12 Santa Clara Computer & High Tech. L. J. 435, 442 (1996). *See generally*, International Finance Corporation, Financing Private Infrastructure (1996).

[2] Andrew D. Cao, *Infrastructure Financing Methods: Paving the Way for Privatization in Latin America*, Latin Finance, Jan. 1993, at 22.

BOT arrangement is a concession agreement by which the host government permits a private party or parties to provide a service to the public in return for payment, while at the same time allowing the government to avoid managerial participation in, financial commitments to, or operating and administrative costs associated with large projects.[3] The private sector participants in a BOT or BOO arrangement organize a special project company and, after obtaining a concession agreement from the government, which is in effect a license form to collect revenue, proceed to construct and operate a facility for a determined period of time, usually between fifteen and twenty-five years, depending on the nature of the project. The precise length of the concession is determined by the estimated time required to obtain sufficient revenue to pay back accrued debt and provide a reasonable return on equity to the investors in the project company. At the end of that period, the private sector participants transfer to the host government the project company or the project assets along with the managerial expertise and technological capability to enable the host government to assume control and effectively operate the project thereafter.

[B] Advantages and Risks of BOT Arrangements

BOT and BOO arrangements have increased rapidly in number and size since the early 1990's because of the advantages they offer to both investors and host country governments. In addition to their advantages, BOTs and BOOs, like any investment also present risks to both parties. This sections examines the advantages and risks for both governments and private investors.

[1] For the Host Government

A key advantage of BOTs and BOOs for host country governments is that these arrangements facilitate the acquisition and efficient operation of modern infrastructure without the need for the host country to provide or raise the necessary capital. Since such projects are based upon nonrecourse project financing, they do not increase government indebtedness, divert government funds from other needed purposes, or require a government guarantee of loans to the project as was usual for infrastructure development in the past. At the same

---

[3] M. L. Hemsley & E. P. White, *The Privatization Experience in Malaysia: Integrating Build-Operate-Own and BOT Techniques within the National Privatization Strategy*, 28 Colum. J. World Bus. 70, 89 (1993).

time, BOTs enable the government to control the development and operation of the project through the concession agreement and also to be assured of complete ownership of the project at some time in the future. Because the BOT arrangement does not make the foreign investor the permanent owner of the facility, some host governments may allow foreign investment in certain sectors only on a BOT basis. China, for example, has a policy which prohibits foreign investors from exclusive operation and control of infrastructure projects that "closely affect the daily lives of the Chinese people."[4] In the power industry, the Chinese government has passed legislation stating "that with the exception of build-operate-transfer projects, a foreign investor generally is not permitted to take more than a 30% equity interest in a power plant."[5]

BOT projects also hold out the prospect to host governments of reducing overall project costs. Since a single private firm or consortium acts as owner, designer, and builder of the project, it has strong incentives to design and construct the facility for efficient, low-cost operations.[6] Because the investor's interest in the BOT project is for only a limited period, they will be motivated to provide quality services and run an efficient operation from the outset of the project in order to recover costs and make a profit as rapidly as possible through consumer revenue. For the same reason, the investor also has a strong interest in transferring management skills and technology effectively to the project to achieve these ends. The same kind of incentives for efficiency and effective technology transfer did not exist under traditional infrastructure development arrangements where the host country contracted with an international construction firm to design and construct the project and then turned it over to the government which would operate it. BOTs also hold certain risks for host countries. The limited liability of project financing offers the risk that it may encourage investors to pursue risky practices at the potential expense of the public. The non-recourse nature of BOTs means that no investor will be subjected to unlimited liability in the event of loan default. Thus, in a telecommunications project, for instance, any problems the investors encounter may be passed on to users and subscribers in the form of long delays in repairing lines,

---

[4] A. C. Lam, *Infrastructure Investment Tips*, China Bus. Rev., Sept. 1994, at 44.

[5] *Id.*

[6] Sozzi, *supra* n.1, at 450.

poor line quality, relatively high communication costs, and network mismanagement. Since a BOT arrangement enables private firms to have control of important infrastructure services for long periods of time, they may continually continually increase the price of their services so that the public ends up paying more than they would have if the government had provided the same service from the outset.

[2] For the Project Company

BOTs are attractive to private investors for several reasons. First, they allow entry to economic sectors, such as power, telecommunications, and transportation that were formerly closed to foreign investors. Because the demand for infrastructure services is so strong and is predicted to grow dramatically in the years ahead in developing countries, appropriately designed projects in the right countries offer the prospect of significant revenues for years to come. While the BOT is in essence a type of contractual joint venture with the host country government, it may be more suitable for foreign market penetration than traditional joint ventures in certain circumstances since the BOT model affords parties the predictability and security of a limited timeframe, while maintaining most of the beneficial elements of traditional joint ventures.

The risks faced by private investors in undertaking a BOT project are more formidable. Completion risk, operation risk, political risk, market and currency risk, and the limited liability nature of non-recourse financing are factors that should make potential investors cautious when considering a BOT arrangement. One may identify each of these risks as follows: Completion risk, or the risk of whether the construction of the BOT project can be completed and brought into operation, is affected by a variety of factors including possible cost overruns, delays, labor problems, technical setbacks, accidents, and natural disasters. During the construction period, it must be remembered, the project is absorbing vast amounts of capital but is not producing any revenue. Operation risk will be affected by the availability of needed inputs such as fuel, the management expertise of the operator, the competence of the work force, and the project's susceptibility to breakdown and environmental degradation. Conflicts of interest among and between investors and host governments can potentially lead to the breakdown of the working relationship between the parties to the BOT project and ultimately reduce the efficiency of operations. Political risks arising under a BOT arrangement include the threat of nationalization of project facilities during the concession period and the host government's arbitrary action in changing the terms of the concession agreement.

For example, in a BOT project for an electrical generation the concession agreement specifies the tariff rate for the sale of electricity to users, a factor that is crucial to shaping the project's financing. If the government later intervenes to lower the tariff, the project could easily become a losing operation. Other forms of political risk include damage to the project due to war, revolution or civil disorder; overt expropriations without compensation; and covert expropriatory actions such as the imposition of confiscatory taxes or royalties, the cancellation of construction licenses or licenses to import project equipment, and the imposition of export prohibitions, price controls, and exchange control regulations.

Market risk refers to the probability that projects will have an assured, stable market for its services. For example, in developing countries, it sometimes happens that the anticipated customers for a toll road or cellular telephone service are not as numerous as the project sponsors expected because low incomes in the country prevent most people from using the infrastructure services to the level the project proponent anticipated originally. Currency risk occurs when the currency of the project's revenue differs from the currency in which the project has been financed. The relative value of the revenue currency to the financing currency may change unfavorably, or the government through exchange control regulations may restrict the ability of the project company to convert its holdings of local currency into foreign currency necessary to pay foreign expenses, service foreign loans, or repatriate profits to investors.

[C] Parties to BOT Arrangements

The two indispensable parties to a BOT contract are the appropriate government agency, on the one hand, and private sector entities on the other.[7] The *government entity* may be a national government agency, such as a host nation's Ministry of Transportation, a government-owned or controlled corporation, or a local government unit, such as a province or municipality. The government agency determines

---

[7] Aleli Angela G. Quirino, *Implementing and Financing BOT Projects: The Philippine Experience*, in Symposium, Private Investments Abroad-Problems and Solutions 5-1, 5-11 (Carol J. Holgren, ed., 1995).

the need for a project and then invites the private sector either partially or wholly to undertake it. The *private sector party* may consist of several different elements participating in various capacities within the BOT arrangement. In most cases, the private sector parties include the project proponent, the contractor, and the facility operator. In addition, lenders such as international commercial banks and financial institutions usually provide the bulk of the capital necessary to construct the facility. Through their loans, they have a contractual relationship with the project. They are discussed in subsection [E], *infra*.

The project proponent or project sponsor is normally the only entity with which the host government has a contractual relationship in connection with the project. The project proponent has the contractual responsibility for the construction and operation of the BOT project, and must make separate contracts with suppliers, contractors, and facility operators. In order to carry out its responsibilities, it must also have adequate financial resources and commitments from financial institutions to to cover the estimated cost of the project.[8] Since many projects are often too large and complex for a single company to handle, several interested private investors may create a joint venture or consortium to undertake it.[9] Generally the investor or investors form a locally incorporated project company to hold project assets and be legally responsible for the project. Such a local project company also serves to isolate project investors from the risks of project liability, and facilitates subsequent transfer of project assets to the host government.[10] Host governments normally require local incorporation in any event since they feel that such incorporation gives them increased ability to control and tax the project. A host government may restrict foreign participation in the project company by requiring a certain percentage of the company to be owned by its own nationals. In the Philippines, for example, projects that require a public utility franchise must at have at least 60 percent Filipino ownership.

The Contractor may or may not be the project proponent, but must be accredited under the laws of the host government to undertake construction and supply equipment for the project. Some host governments may place special conditions on foreign contractors, for example

---

[8] *Id.*

[9] 2A Philip Wood, Law and Practice of International Finance s. 14.02[1] (1990).

[10] *Id.*

by requiring that local labor be employed in the construction process. Before entering into a concession agreement, the host government may require the project proponent to identify the contractor who will undertake project construction.[11]

The Facility Operator may or may not be the project proponent, and is responsible for all aspects of operation and maintenance of the infrastructure, including the collection of tolls or fees from users. As with the contractor and project company, the host government may require the facility operator to have a certain percentage of local equity ownership.

[D] Approval Process for BOT Projects

Because infrastructure projects involve the provision of a public service and may entail a monopoly over that service, BOT infrastructure projects always require government approval. After identifying priority projects to be implemented under BOT arrangements, the concerned government agency will normally publicize and request bids for its infrastructure project needs, often by publication in national or international newspapers or magazines. Foreign investors may obtain government approval of a BOT project in one of three ways:

1. by international competitive bidding, which accounts for the majority of project approvals;

2. by competitive negotiation, where the government following the announcement of its interest, selects several short-listed bidders using particular criteria and then negotiates with each; and

3. by direct negotiation, which may be initiated by the government or by an investor with an unsolicited proposal.[12]

The process of public bidding is usually begun with the publication by the host government of a notice or invitation to prequalify and bid upon a designated project. The notice states the deadline for submission of prequalification statements and the qualifications that project participants, such as the contractor or facility operator, must have to be pre-identified for pre-qualification purposes.[13] The government

---

[11] Quirino, *supra* n.7, at 5-11.

[12] International Finance Corporation, *Financing Private Infrastructure* 48-50 (1996).

[13] Quirino, *supra* n.7, at 5-15.

agency overseeing the approval process makes available to interested investors the bid/tender documents to serve as guidelines for the preparation of prequalification applications and bid proposals. These documents may include: instructions to bidders, minimum design and performance standards and specifications, economic parameters, draft contracts, bid forms, forms of bid and performance securities, and any other materials considered necessary by the government agency. Prospective bidders are given a specified period of time from the last date of publication of the notice to prepare and submit these documents to the host government. Among other things, they should state the bidder's compliance with legal requirements, experience and technological expertise, and financial credibility. After possible pre-bid conferences with the host government agency to clarify any provisions of the bid documents, private investors typically submit both a "technical proposal" and a "financial proposal.

Under the Philippine bidding procedure, for example, the government employs a two-envelope/two-stage evaluation system. In the first stage, only the "Technical proposals" submitted in the first envelopes are opened to ascertain whether they are complete with all necessary data and bid securities. The second envelopes containing "Financial proposals" are returned unopened to bidders disqualified because of incomplete data. In the second stage, the second envelopes of bidders who passed the first stage are be opened for further consideration. BOT projects are generally awarded to the bidder who has submitted the lowest bid and the most favorable terms for the project. Unsolicited proposals may be accepted by the host government agency on a negotiated basis under certain circumstances. These circumstances may include the existence of new technology or a concept that the host government has not identified as a priority project; a proposal not requiring a direct government guarantee, subsidy or equity; or a situation where the host government receives an attractive proposal after failing to receive any bids in response to its original published invitation.[14] A host government may also engage in direct negotiations with a potential investor in cases where the government has only one qualifying bidder for the designated project, either because it received no other bids or because all other bids did not meet the prequalification or proposal requirements. In some countries, for example the Philippines, a disqualified bidder may be able to appeal the

---

[14] *Id.* at 5-17.

decision of disqualification to the head of the government agency.[15] After the winning bidder is notified, the parties are given a short period of time to execute the concession contract. In the event of refusal, inability or failure by the winning bidder to execute the contract, it forfeits its bid security. The next lowest complying and qualified evaluated bid is then considered. The project may be subject to rebidding if either the government or the bidder refuses to execute a contract.[16]

[E] Financing of BOT Projects

After approval of the project and execution of the a concession agreement, the project company will then make contracts with equipment suppliers, a construction contractor, and an operations and maintenance contractor. Under the BOT scheme, the project company or consortium has the responsibility of securing the necessary financing for construction of the project. In addition to the equity contributed by investors in the project company, sources of finance include loans from commercial banks, leasing companies, insurance companies, pension funds, governmental bond authorities, and bilateral and multilateral lending institutions. Export credit agencies often provide credit guarantees. Like most project financing schemes, BOT project financing is predicated on the merits of a project rather than the credit of the project sponsor. Lenders to the project base their credit appraisal on the expected cash flow from the contemplated revenues of the project, independent of the credit worthiness of the project sponsor. Moreover, the debt is non-recourse, so that the project sponsor has no direct legal obligation to repay the project loans or make interest payments if the cash flows prove inadequate to service debt.[17] Such "project specific" lending often enables developing countries to receive more favorable credit terms than they might otherwise obtain in circumstances where political upheaval or a history of debt default has caused lenders to view such countries as high credit risks.[18]

---

[15] Philippine Republic Act No. 7718 s. 5-A, Implementing R. & Regs. R. 10.

[16] Quirino, *Implementing and Financing BOT Projects: The Philippine Experience*, in Symposium, Private Investments Abroad-Problems and Solutions 5-1, 5-18 (Carol J. Holgren, ed., 1995).

[17] Scott L. Hoffman, *A Practical Guide to Transactional Project Finance: Basic Concepts, Risk Identification, and Contractual Considerations*, 45 Bus. Law. 181, 182-83 (1989).

[18] Sozzi, *Comment: Project Finance and Facilitating Telecommunications Infrastructure Development in Newly-Industrializing Countries*, 12 Santa Clara Computer & High Tech. L. J. 435, 480 (1996).

Because the ability of the project sponsor to produce revenue from project operations is the foundation of BOT financing, the BOT legal and contractual framework has an important impact on project viability and the allocation of risks.[19] BOT project financing requires a predictable regulatory and political environment and a stable market to produce dependable cash flow. To the extent this predictability is questionable, lenders may require credit enhancement to protect them from external uncertainties and changes in law. Lenders may receive security in the form of guarantees by investors or others of loans to the project company, the pledge of shares in the project company, an assignment of rights from the project agreement, and the mortgage of assets. The lenders must be persuaded that for the term of BOT contract, project cash flow will be sufficient to cover costs and repay the loans on schedule and before transfer of the facility to the host government.[20] The concession agreement provides the basis for revenues payable to the project company. The project company may be repaid in the form of tolls and fees, a share in revenues, or nonmonetary payments, such as a portion of the land reclaimed by the government. The tolls and fees that may be charged are set at levels that allow the project proponent to recover its total investments and the costs of operations and maintenance, and to obtain a reasonable rate of return on investments and operating and maintenance costs. The tolls and fees are subject to adjustment during the life of the contract, based on a predetermined formula using official price indices.[21]

[F] Legal Framework of BOT Arrangements

The legal framework for a BOT project consists of the relevant host country legislation, its system of regulations, the concession agreement between the host country agency and the project company, and the various contracts between the project company and its lenders, contractors, suppliers and others necessary for the project. Although the concession agreement stipulates key provisions governing the relationship between the host country and the project company, the source of many of those concession provisions is set out in the law and regulations of the host country. For example, the law may place

---

[19] Hoffman, *supra* n.17, at 183.
[20] Quirino, *supra* n.16, at 5-23.
[21] *Id.* at 5-14.

maximum limits on the rate of return permitted to the project company. National legislation may also specify certain privileges and guarantees to be enjoyed by BOT projects and provide a framework for the enforcement of contractual obligations. One important issue is the existence of a reliable mechanism ensuring that earnings in local currency can be converted into foreign currency and repatriated.[22] For example, Vietnam's BOT Regulation states: "The government shall guarantee that the revenue received by the BOT company during this period of operation be converted from Vietnamese currency into foreign currencies in accordance with the contract for the purposes of repaying loan capital and interest, paying all expenditure requiring foreign currency and paying to foreign investors their share of profits which are transferred abroad."[23]

A host government may regulate concession agreements either through special legislation or through ordinary contract and administrative law. Turkey, for example, passed legislation in 1994 attempting to ensure the effective implementation of BOT arrangements by delineating the process for awarding contracts to local joint stock and foreign companies that want to provide capital investment or services under BOT arrangements. It also stipulated the BOT approval process and the required characteristics of companies seeking to participate in BOT projects, including technical qualifications and investment and capitalization ratios.[24] This legislation also sought to remove Turkish BOT projects from the realm of concession agreements, since aggrieved private parties to concessions under Turkish law can only adjudicate their claims in Turkish courts and may not have recourse to international arbitration. The 1994 law declared BOT agreements to be commercial contracts, which can be arbitrated internationally and which therefore would give investors greater assurance of a neutral and impartial dispute resolution process in any dispute with the Turkish government in connection with a BOT arrangement. Unfortunately, the Turkish Constitutional Court decided in a 1996 case that BOT projects are concessions, not commercial contracts, and therefore fall under the laws and regulations governing concessions. The effect of this ruling is to give Turkish administrative courts exclusive jurisdiction over BOT disputes.[25] Several countries have also enacted

---

[22] Ian Arstall & David Platt, Project Finance, Int'l Fin. L. Rev., Feb. 1995, at 27.

[23] *Id.*

[24] Sozzi, *supra* n.18, at 465-66.

[25] *Id.* at 466.

codes governing concessions within particular industries and sectors. These codes may establish requirements concerning ownership of resources, state participation in the operation of the project, taxation of project revenues, regulation of project operations, maximum rates of return, and bidding procedures for award of a BOT projects.[26] An important issue with respect to the BOT legal framework concerns the status to be accorded to the concession agreement under host country law. A concession agreement has a dual nature as both contract and an act of the sovereign. The world's legal systems view concession agreements in different ways.[27] Countries based on the common law tradition distinguish between private and government contracts. Traditionally, under such legal regimes, contractual and tort remedies are available only for breaches that arise under private contracts. A private party to a government contract may not sue the government if the government breaches the contract, unless there is an express provision in the law granting recourse. Thus, a host government might permit suits either explicitly in the concession agreement or in the law.[28]

The two main branches of the civil law tradition, the French and German legal systems, treat concessions differently. French Civil law considers a concession agreement as a "contrat administratif," rather than private law agreement. "French administrative law, with a well developed body of doctrine on administrative contracts, treats the parties thereto unequally and allows the state or its contracting instrumentality to alter the provisions of an administrative contract unilaterally.[29]

German civil law considers the grant of a concession or license as a unilateral administrative act and makes no distinction between private and government contracts. The contract merely describes the relationship between the concessionaire and the government. The German legal system, therefore, considers a concession agreement's binding power as predicated "upon the existence of a valid administrative act."[30]

---

[26] Viktor Soloveytchik, *New Perspectives For Concession Agreements*, 16 Hous. J. Int'l L. 261, 267 (1993).

[27] *Id.*

[28] *Id.*

[29] *Id.* at 264-65.

[30] *Id.*

For the foreign investor in a BOT arrangement, a key concern is the stability and enforceability of the concession agreement. Once having entered into a concession agreement, to what extent can the host government change its terms by unilateral action or by enacting laws that obstruct the operation of the project or place more onerous burdens on it than were contemplated at the time the concession agreement's execution? In order to protect themselves against such eventuality, foreign investors often insist that concession agreements contain special commitments not to expropriate the project, guarantees on repatriation of profits and convertibility of project revenues, and stabilization clauses stipulating that future changes in legislation will not impose more onerous conditions on the project that those that existed at the time the concession agreement was executed. Chapter 27, *infra*, discusses at length the use of such protective agreements with the host country government.

Even where the contractual language is clear, the basic problem with respect to such protective agreements is whether a sovereign state can bind itself in a contract not to use its sovereign powers to change it later on. From a theoretical point of view, some scholars argue that a state cannot effectively bind itself not to expropriate property or change concession agreements in the future since the power to expropriate or modify state contract stems from its power of eminent domain and is an inherent part of its sovereignty. Since its purpose as a sovereign state is to secure the public interest of its citizens and to safeguard their welfare, the state must remain free to exercise its right of eminent domain when circumstances so require.[31] To give up the power to expropriate private property would be to give up its status as a sovereign state.

Moreover, if a contract is a creature of host country law, the host country should be able to alter that contract by a subsequent law. It is often held that the legislative power of a sovereign state cannot be limited by a contractual provision, particularly where such legislation is for the public benefit.[32] Moreover, as noted above, many legal systems in the industrialized world allow the government under certain

---

[31] Ingrid Delupis, Finance and Protection of Investments in Developing Countries 31 (1973).

[32] M. Sornarajah, The International Law on Foreign Investment 331 (1994).

conditions to interfere with contracts in the public interest in certain situations.[33]

In order to meet these theoretical and practical limitations on the use of contractual provisions to protect investments, foreign investors have sought to develop devices to "internationalize" such contracts, to take them out of the purview of host country law and make them subject to international law. In short, they have sought to use contracts and international law to restrain the legislative power of sovereign states as a means to protect their investments abroad.

Specifically, such protective measures include contractual provisions on (a) the choice of the applicable law so as to remove the contract from host country law, (b) international dispute settlement to remove any resulting conflict from the jurisdiction of host country courts, (c) waiver of sovereign immunity, and (d) waiver of the requirement that the investor first exhaust local remedies for investment disputes before seeking other forms of redress. The devices are discussed at length in section 27.02, infra.

So long as BOT concession agreements are governed by the law of the host country, the host country government—by virtue of its sovereign legislative and executive powers—has the power to amend or nullify such contractual provisions and guarantees in its unilateral discretion. As a result, the durability of such contractual provisions may appear doubtful to the foreign investor.

In order to isolate the contract from future undesirable changes in the law of the host country, the investor may seek to include a provision in the contract which subjects the agreement to a body of law other than that of the host country.[34] Although the validity of

---

[33] Patrick M. Norton, *A Law of the Future or A Law of The Past? Modern Tribunals and the International Law of Expropriation*, 85 American J. Int'l L. 474,493 (1991). See also M. Sornarajah, *The International Law on Foreign Investment* 344 (1994), who claims there is a basis for arguing that state contracts with private parties are universally recognized as defeasible in the public interest and that no illegality can be attached to its breach by the state if such breach is for a public purpose.

[34] Roland Brown, *Choice of Law in Concession and Related Contracts*, 39 Mod. L. Rev. 625 (1976). *See also* George A. Bermann, *Contracts Between States and Foreign Nationals: A Reassessment* in *International Contracts* 183-195 (Smit, Galston, and Levitsky eds. 1981). *See* Charles Nelson Brower, *International Legal Protection of United States Investment Abroad* in 3 *A Lawyer's Guide to International Business Transactions* 30-34 (W. Surrey & D. Wallace 2d ed. 1981). For a detailed discussion of choice of law provisions, see ch. 30, *Planning for Dispute Settlement*

this approach was challenged at one time on the assumption that a contract between a state and a foreign national had to be governed by the state's municipal law, it is now generally agreed that the parties to the agreement may choose another law to govern its provisions.[35] Theoretically, the range of choices open to the parties is broad and may include: the domestic law of the investor's home country; the domestic law of a third country; international law; "general principles of law"; legal principles common to the legal systems of both parties; or some combination of any of the preceding choices.[36] Rather than selecting a law outside the host country, an alternative method of seeking to inhibit the host country's legislative discretion is to provide that the agreement shall be governed by the law of the host country *as of a certain date*—normally the date of the execution of the contract itself.[37] The effect of such provisions, it is often said, is to "stabilize" the law of the host country. Hence these provisions are known as stabilization clauses. Such stabilization clauses have been held to be valid and enforceable;[38] however, some scholars have argued that legally the power of the state to legislate cannot be restrained by a simple contract.[39]

Despite the breadth of the *theoretical* range of choices concerning the law applicable to an investment or economic development

---

in *International Business Transactions*. In earlier times, another reason for choosing foreign law to govern the concession agreement was that the law of the host country was vague, uncertain, or unfavorable with respect to important questions affecting the investment project.

[35] Bermann, *supra*, n.34 at 187-189. But see M. Sornarajah, *The International law on Foreign Investment* 332-334 (1994) for a contrary view. It may be noted that Article 42(l) of the World Bank Convention on the Settlement of Investment Disputes between States and Nationals of Other States, 17 U.S.T. 1270, T.I.A.S. No. 6090, 575 U.N.T.S. 159, provides as follows: "The tribunal shall decide a dispute in accordance with such rules of law as may be agreed by the parties. In the absence of such agreement, the tribunal shall apply the law of the contracting state party to the dispute (including its rules on the conflict of laws) and such rules of international law as may be applicable." For a discussion of the Convention and the International Centre for Settlement of Investment Disputes see ch. 31, *International Commercial Arbitration*.

[36] George van Hecke, *Contracts Subject to International or Transnational Law* in *International Contracts* 26-28 (Smit, Galston, and Levitsky eds. 1981).

[37] Brown, *supra* n.29, at 628. *See also* E. Paasivirta, *Internationalization and Stabilization of Contracts Versus State Sovereignty*, 50 British Yearbook of International Law 315 (1989).

[38] *See, e.g., Aminoil v. Kuwait* 21 I.L.M. 976 (1982).

[39] M. Sornarajah, The International Law on Foreign Investment 328-32 (1994).

agreement, the foreign investor has relatively few real choices in practice. Although a foreign investor in former days might have been able to impose a foreign law on the contract, in today's world of heightened economic and political nationalism few host country governments would accept a foreign law provision. As a result, the vast majority of choice of law provisions in concession and economic development and investment agreements today provide that the applicable law shall be that of the host country.[40]

While a host country may categorically refuse to accept a provision applying foreign law, it may, under certain circumstances, agree to the application of international law or general international principles to the agreement. Although international law may be vague on many points, it does offer the investor protection which may be superior to that offered by the legal system of the host country. For one thing, as will be seen in § 27.04 below, traditional principals of international law require the host country to pay "prompt, adequate, and effective compensation" in the event of expropriation. For another, the maxim *pacta sunt servanda*—that contracts are to be performed—is generally considered a fundamental principle of international law.[41] This principle can be applied to require a state to respect its contractual obligations to a foreign national where such obligations are embodied in agreements specifically subjected to international law. For example, in arbitrations rising out of Libya's nationalization of foreign oil interests and its repudiation of related obligations embodied in deeds and concessions with the nationalized parties, three separate international arbitrations applied the principle of *pacta sunt servanda* to the Libyan agreements and held Libya liable for its failure to respect its commitments.[42]

Choice of law provisions which seek to "internationalize" concession and investment contracts between the host country and the foreign investor may refer only to international law, or "the general principles of law," or they may provide for the application of some combination

---

[40] Georges R. Delaume, *State Contracts and Transnational Arbitration*, 75 Am. J. Int'l L. 784, 796 (1981).

[41] *See, e.g.*, Gormley, *The Codification of Pacta Sunt Servanda by the International Law Commission*, 14 St. Louis U.L.J. 367, 371-75 (1970). *See generally* Hans Wehberg, *Pact Sunt Servanda*, 53 Am. J. Int'l L. 775-786 (1959).

[42] *See* Robert B. von Mehren & Nicholas Kourides, *International Arbitrations Between States and Foreign Private Parties: The Libyan Nationalization Cases*, 75 Am. J. Int'l L. 476 513-515 (1981).

of domestic and international law. For example, the choice of law provision applied in the Libyan arbitration cases provided that the applicable law was to be the "principles of law of Libya common to the principles of international law and in the absence of such common principles then by and in accordance with the general principles of law, including such of those principles as may have been applied by international tribunals."[43]

If the agreement between the state and a foreign investor makes no specific reference to a governing law, it is possible, in certain circumstances, that an international tribunal may ultimately find that the parties had implicitly subjected the agreement to international law. For example, one arbitration award indicated that a factor suggesting that the parties intended international law to govern their contract was a clause providing for the resolution of disputes by international arbitration.[44] Moreover, in an arbitration arising out of the imposition of taxes on a foreign investment project in violation of a promise by the Jamaican government that no additional taxes or levies would be imposed, the majority of the tribunal found that, even though the agreement had no specific choice-of-law clause, it was not to be governed exclusively by Jamaican law. The majority of the arbitration panel stated: "Although the agreement was silent as to the applicable law, we accept Jamaican law for all ordinary purposes of the agreement, but we do not consider that its applicability for some purposes precludes the application of principles of public international law which govern the responsibility of states for injuries to aliens. We regard these principles as particularly applicable where the question is, as here, whether actions taken by a government contrary to and damaging to the economic interests of aliens are in conflict with understandings and assurances given in good faith to such aliens as an inducement to their making the investments affected by the action."[45]

Although theoretical questions remain about the stability of concession agreements, foreign investors would be well advised to include in their BOT agreements stabilization clauses that provide that existing law at the time of the execution of the contract will continue to apply

---

[43] *Id.* at 497-500.

[44] Delaume, *supra* n.40, at 798-801.

[45] Revere Copper & Brass, Inc. v. Overseas Private Investment Corp. (OPIC), 17 Int'l Legal Mat. 1321, 1331 (1978).

and that future laws and regulations placing increased burdens on the project will be inapplicable; that the concession agreement will be subject to international law and practice, general principles of law, or the law of a third country; and that all disputes between the investors and the host government with respect the the concession agreement will be settled by international arbitration. The practice of international arbitral tribunals strongly indicates that such provisions will be respected and therefore give stability to the concession agreement. Such contractual provisions are very important to BOT projects because of the somewhat uncertain nature of concession agreements and lack of a cohesive international regime governing BOTs. Let us next examine the provisions of the concession agreement itself.

[G] The BOT Concession Agreement

The concession agreement between the host government and the project company is the legal heart of any BOT arrangement. It establishes the respective legal rights and obligations of the parties and provides the license for construction and operation of the project. It will also influence the kinds of other agreements, such as the construction contract, loans, company charter, and operating contracts that the project company will have to negotiate with other parties in order to contract and operate the infrastructure facility. Among the issues normally treated in a concession agreement are the following:

1. Concession Rights and Obligations

The contract should define what is required of the concession operator, what precisely the operator will be permitted to do and the length of time for which the concession is granted.[46] This section of the agreement states the general rights and obligations granted to the concessionaire and usually that the concessionaire has the responsibility to undertake them at its own expense and risk, without government financial credits or guarantees. The provision may also deal with concession fees to be paid to the government, land ownership arrangements and any related works that the government may be required to provide in the area in support of the BOT project.

2. The Project Company.

---

[46] Sozzi, *Comment: Project Finance and Facilitating Telecommunications Infrastructure Development in Newly-Industrializing Countries*, 12 Santa Clara Computer & High Tech. L. J. 435, 471.

The concession agreement often stipulates the capital and other requirements of the project company, and may even set out its corporate charter, including provisions on capital structure, restrictions on foreign ownership and control, internal organization and management, and the organization of the board of directors.

3. Timing

Since the development of a large infrastructure facility is a complex and lengthy process, the concession agreement will usually stipulate dates for the completion of various phases in making the BOT project a reality.

4. Site Acquisition

Often the government has the responsibility to acquire the land for the BOT facility. The concession agreement will specify the government's obligations in this regard and the nature of the rights to be transferred to the project company under the concession.

5. Appointment of an Independent Engineer

The concession usually provides for the appointment of an independent engineer during the construction phase, and possibly thereafter, to report to the government, the concession company and the lenders on the work being done. The independent engineer has the responsibility to inspect the facility upon completion of construction and to certify that it meets construction contract specifications.

6. Fees, Tolls, and Compensation

The agreement will specify the fees and tolls to be charged by the concession company for the use of the facility and will usually incorporate a formula or set of principles governing fee and toll increases in the future. To assure that the project company operates the facility in an efficient manner, concession agreements often link payments to required performance levels, such as minimum power availability, the number of new water or telephone connections, toll road and bridge capacity, and fault repair times. The agreement may state that if the project company fails to meet specified performance criteria it will have to pay certain penalties to the host government.

7. Operation and Maintenance

This provision specifies the nature of the project company's obligations in connection with the operation and maintenance of the facility.

8. Profit Sharing and Other Payments to the Government

Often the Concession agreement will stipulate payment of a portion of the profits or revenues from the project to the government.

Additional issues that may arise in negotiating a concession agreement include: whether the host government is to be compensated through royalty payments and taxation or by an equity share in the project company; whether the project company will be subject to existing price controls or mandatory local sale requirements; and whether the company will be permitted to freely import foreign materials and equipment supplies free of customs duties. It may also be necessary to include renewal provisions to facilitate future restructuring if the parties decide to extend the concession period in the future.[47]

The investors in the project may seek additional legal security through provisions on force majeure, tax reassessments, government guarantees on convertibility of local currency for repatriation of capital and profits, and payment of debt service and purchase of needed imports, and the right of the project company to freely manage the project without government interference. Project sponsors, as discussed above, also seek stabilization clauses and specific provisions against the expropriation and nationalization of the project prior to its natural termination. Such provisions should clearly define the activities that will constitute a "nationalization" by the government. In Thailand in 1995, for example, a highway project encountered this issue when the parties failed to agree as to whether the Thai government's forcing open of a toll road, prior to completing a specific agreement on revenue-sharing and other matters, constituted a "nationalization" of the project. Since a project company requires a 20 to 30 year concession period in which to recover its costs and repay its lenders, the earlier the termination by governmental action the greater would be the government's liability in damages in the event of such a breach of the concession agreement.[48]

In addition to these key provisions, concession agreements may contain a variety of annexes on such matters as project design

---

[47] *Id* at 472.

[48] Paul A. Sherer, *Mass-Transit Mystery: Bangkok Begins Building As-Yet Unfunded Railway*, Asian Wall St. J. Wkly., May 1, 1995, at 1.

procedures, principle terms to be included in the construction contract, guarantee bonds, and environmental permits and requirements.[49]

[H] Other Contracts

The project sponsor enters into a variety of other contracts in order to carry out the BOT facility contemplated by the concession agreement. These agreement include the following:

[1] Consortium Agreement

The project company may be controlled by a consortium, comprised of investors, construction companies, consultants, financiers and equipment suppliers, as well as the host government if it chooses to participate in the project company through ownership of a portion of the equity. In the event such a consortium of participants exists, they will usually conclude a consortium agreement to determine their respective rights and obligations, to regulate the relationship among them, and to guide the day-to-day management of the company. The consortium contract states funding responsibilities and levels of shareholding, as well as any restrictions on share transfer. It may also include a detailed liquidation procedure in the event the project fails prior to its transfer to the host government. The consortium's charter documents also address issues such as share capital, number and appointment of directors, requirements regarding loan finance, appointment of financial and legal advisors, access to accounting records, confidentiality, dividend policy, share transfers, debt servicing, governing law, service of process, and resolution of disputes.[50]

[2] The Project Company

The project company may take one of a several of legal organizational forms: a wholly owned subsidiary, general partnership, limited partnership, joint venture or limited liability company. The choice as to which form to use will depend on an analysis of many factors including taxation, local law requirements, demands of lenders, operating convenience, and business objectives of the parties, among others. For example, some countries may not allow complete foreign ownership of corporate entities or may restrict foreigners from owning

---

[49] For an outline of basic terms in toll road concession agreements and power purchase agreements, see International Finance Corporation, Financing Private Infrastructure 112-126 (1996).

[50] Sozzi, *supra* n.46, at 474.

certain common carrier facilities. Moreover, the host government may seek to retain some control over the company during the concession operation, but at the same time may not be able or willing to be an equity participant in the project. In such cases, a partnership or contractual joint venture may be an appropriate legal form. On the other hand, a limited partnership, under which each "limited partner" shares in the project profits while enjoying limited liability, may permit capital contributions by passive project investors, such as contractors and equipment suppliers, while giving them certain tax advantages.

[3] The Construction Agreement

The project company will generally seek to enter into a fixed-price, lump-sum turnkey contract for the construction of the facility so as to fix an important portion of project costs and hedge completion risks. Completion delays cost overruns, and the failure of the completed facility to perform according to expectations are some of the main uncertainties associated with construction risk. The construction contract will seek to deal with these problems by clearly specifying dates and performance standards, and it will include liquidated damages provisions for late completion or failure to meet guaranteed performance. The construction contractor will also be required to provide a project completion performance bond from a reliable bonding company to compensate the project company and the host country for failure to complete the project on time because of bankruptcy, default, labor strikes or natural disasters. In some cases, where completion bonds are unavailable, the contractor may be required to provide a standby letter of credit from a recognized international commercial bank. Other construction risks that should be considered in the contract are price changes caused by currency fluctuations or inflation, material shortages, design changes required by law, and labor disputes.[51]

[4] Operations and Management Agreement

The project company may entrust management of the facility to another party, in which case the companies will enter into an operations and management agreement. In addition to receiving fixed operations/management fees from the pool of incoming revenues, the

---

[51] Sozzi, *supra* n.46, at 482. *See also* International Finance Corporation, Financing Private Infrastructure 69-70 (1996).

operator may be remunerated through incentive payments designed to encourage superior levels of performance and may also be obligated to pay penalties if performance does not meet stipulated standards.

The host government may seek to retain some control over the project to ensure efficient operation of the facilities. Toward this end, the contract may provide for the assignability of an operator's obligations and rights by the government so as to allow the removal of ineffective operators in the event of certain predetermined contingencies, such as inadequate revenue, failing technology, or poor service quality. Another relevant issue that should be provided for within the Operations & Management contract is indemnification. The contracting agency or the host government will usually wish to be protected against all liabilities and claims resulting from the project company's operation of the project.

[5] Loan Agreements

A major portion of the funding for BOT infrastructure projects comes from lenders of varying sorts. These loans are of course supported by loan agreements. In order to protect themselves from the considerable risks entailed by infrastructure project, lenders normally require their loan documents to include numerous loan covenants stipulating how the borrower (i.e. the project company) will use the funds and manage the project. Such loan covenants may include provisions on minimum debt service ratio, a measure of a project's debt service obligations relative to its cash flow. Covenants may also prohibit the payment of dividends to investors if the current ratio falls below a stated amount, and limit capital expenditures to a maximum amount per year. To assure payment of debt service, the loan agreement may require the establishment of debt reserve accounts of a fixed amount to insure that debt servicing will continue uninterrupted if there is a fall in project revenues. Lenders may even require that debt reserve accounts be held off-shore in an established financial institution, to avoid the risk of possible intervention by the host government to prevent its use.

Selected Bibliography

I. Direct Foreign Investment

A. Generally

Aharoni, Yair, *The Foreign Investment Decision Process* (1966).

Black, Robert, Stephen Blank and Elizabeth Hanson, *Multinationals in Contention: Responses at Governmental and International Levels* (1978).

Boarman, P., and H. Schollhammer, eds., *Multinational Corporations and Governments: Business-Government Relations in an International Context* (1975).

Brower, Charles Nelson, "International Legal Protection of United States Investment Abroad," in 3 *A Lawyer's Guide to International Business Transactions*, Folio 6 (Walter Sterling Surrey and Don Wallace, Jr., eds. 2d ed. 1981).

Chan, Steve, *Foreign Direct Investment in Changing Global Political Economy* (1995).

Fatouros, A.A., *Government Guarantees to Foreign Investors* (1962).

Froot, Kenneth A.(ed), Foreign Direct Investment (1993).

Grove, Stephen, ed., *Legal Aspects of International Investment* (1977).

Hahlo, H., J. Smith and R. Wright, eds., *Nationalism and the Multinational Enterprise: Legal, Economic and Managerial Aspects* (1973).

Kindleberger, Charles P., *American Business Abroad: Six Lectures on Direct Investment* (1969).

Kindleberger, Charles P., ed., *The International Corporation* (1970).

Kojima, Kiyoshi, *Direct Foreign Investment: A Japanese Model of Multinational Business Operations* (1978).

Kuusi, Juha, *The Host State and the Transnational Corporation: An Analysis of Legal Relationships* (1979).

LaFave, Wayne R. and Peter Hay, eds., *International Trade, Investment and Organization* (1967).

Lowenfeld, Andreas F., *International Private Investment* (1976).

Modelski, G., ed., *Transnational Corporations and World Order: Readings in International Political Economy* (1979).

Oxelheim, Lars (ed.), *The Global Race for Direct Foreign Investment: Prospects For the Future* (1993).

Practicing Law Institute. *The U.S.-Based Corporation Expanding into the International Arena* (1976; 1978).

Quirino, Aleli Angela G., *Implementing and Financing BOT Projects: The Philippine Experience*, in Symposium, Private Investments Abroad-Problems and Solutions 5-1, 5-11 (Carol J. Holgren, ed., 1995).

Root, Franklin, *Foreign Market Entry Strategies* (1982).

Rugman, Alan M., *International Diversification and the Multinational Enterprise* (1979).

Safarian, A. E., *Multinational Enterprise & Public Policy: A Study of the Industrial Countries* (1992).

Sornarajah, M., *The International Law on Foreign Investment* (1994).

Sozzi, Christopher J., *Comment: Project Finance and Facilitating Telecommunications Infrastructure Development in Newly-Industrializing Countries*, 12 Santa Clara Computer & High Tech. L. J. 435 (1996).

U.S. Department of Commerce, *Foreign Investment and Licensing Checklist for U.S. Firms* (rev. Oct. 1981).

Wallace, Don., Jr., *International Regulation of Multinational Corporations* (1976).

Young, John H., "Establishing and Financing a Foreign Enterprise," 1976 *Tax Mgmt. Int'l J.* 76–11, 14 (1976).

B. Treaty Framework

International Chamber of Commerce, *Bilateral Treaties for International Investment* (1977).

International Chamber of Commerce (U.S. Council), *Rights of Businessmen Abroad Under Trade Agreements and Commercial Treaties* (1960).

Malecek, Robert M., "United States Bilateral Non-Tariff Commercial Treaty Practice: A Section Membership Survey," 10 *Int'l Law.* 561 (1976).

Norton, "The Renegotiability of United States Bilateral Commercial Treaties With the Member States of the European Economic Community," 8 *Tex. Int'l L.J.* 299 (1973).

Salacuse, Jeswald W., "BIT By BIT: The Growth of Bilateral Investment Treaties and Their Impact on Foreign Investment in Developing Countries," 24 The Int'l Lawyer 655-675(1990).

Salacuse, Jeswald W., "Towards a New Treaty Framework for Direct Foreign Investment," 50 *J. Air L. & Com.* 969 (1985).

Walker, "Modern Treaties of Friendship, Commerce and Navigation," 42 *Minn. L. Rev.* 805 (1958).

Walker, "The Post-War Commercial Treaty Program of the United States," 73 *Pol. Sci. Qtr.* 57 (1958).

Walker, "Provisions on Companies in United States Commercial Treaties," 50 *Am. J. Int'l L.* 373 (1956).

Wilson, Robert R., *United States Commercial Treaties and International Law* (1960).

C. Developing Countries

Andersson, Thomas, *Multinational Investment in Developing Countries: A Study of Taxation & Nationalization* (1991).

Comment, "Multinational Corporations and Lesser Developed Countries—Foreign Investment, Transfer of Technology, and the Paris Convention: Caveat Investor," 5 *U.Dayton L. Rev.* 105 (1980).

Farer, Tom J., "Economic Development Agreements: A Functional Analysis," 10 *Colum. J. Transnat'l L.* 200 (1971).

Foreign Investment, International Law and National Development (Seventh Waigani Seminar, J. Zorn and P. Bayne eds. 1973).

Frank, Isaiah, *Foreign Investment in Developing-Countries* (1980).

Hellawell, Robert and Don Wallace, Jr., eds., *Negotiating Foreign Investments: A Manual for the Third World* (2 vols. 1982).

Investing, Licensing and Trading Conditions Abroad (Business International Corporation, 1982).

Kurian, George Thomas, *Encyclopedia of the Third World* (rev. ed. 3 vols. 1982).

Lall, Sanjaya and Paul Streeten, *Foreign Investment, Transnationals, and Developing Countries* (1977).

LaPalombara, Joseph and Stephen Blank, *Multinational Corporations and Developing Countries* (1979).

Organization for Economic Co-operation and Development, *Investing in Developing Countries* (4th rev. ed. 1978).

OECD, *Promoting Foreign Direct Investment in Developing Countries* (1993).

Robinson, Richard D., *Foreign Investment in the Third World: A Comparative Study of Selected Developing Country Investment Promotion Programs* (International Division, U.S. Chamber of Commerce 1980).

Sinha, S. Prakash, *New Nations and the Law of Nations* (1967).

D. Industrialized Countries

Grewlich, Klaus W., *Direct Investment in the OECD Countries* (1978).

Organization for Economic Co-operation and Development, *Code of Liberalization of Capital Movements* (August, 1973, updated, June 1978).

Olson, Thomas H., "Foreign Investment Restrictions on Canadian Energy Resources," 14 *Int'l Law.* 579 (1980).

E. Political Risk

Gomes-Casseres, Benjamin & Yoffie, David B., *The International Political Economy of Direct Foreign Investment (2 vols.) (1993)*.

Green, Robert T., *Political Instability as a Determinant of U.S. Foreign Investment* (1972).

Haendel, Don, *Foreign Investments and the Management of Political Risk* (1979).

Kobrin, Stephen J., "Political Risk: A Review and Reconsideration," 10 *J. Int'l Bus. Stud.* 69 (Spring/Summer 1979).

Rummel, R.J., and David A. Heenan, "How Multinationals Analyze Political Risk," 56 *Harv. Bus. Rev.* 67 (January/February 1978).

Thunell, Lars H., *Political Risks in International Business: Investment Behavior of Multinational Corporations* (1977).

F. Privatization

Berenson, William M. *Legal Considerations and the Role of Lawyers in the Privatization Process: An Overview*, 37 Fed. B. News & J. 159 (March/April 1990).

Ernst & Young, *Privatization: Investing in Infrastructures Around the World* (1994).

Nankani, Helen. Techniques of Privatization of State-Owned Enterprises, Volume II, Selected Country Case Studies, (World Bank Technical Paper Number 89, 1988).

Candoye-Sekse, Rebecca, Techniques of Privatization of State-Owned Enterprises, Volume III, Inventory of Country Experience and Reference Materials (World Bank Technical Paper Number 90, 1988).

Ramamurti, Ravi. *Why are Developing Countries Privatizing?*, in 23 J. of Int'l Bus. Stud. 225 (1992).

Vuylsteke, Charles. Techniques of Privatization of State-Owned Enterprise, Volume I, Methods and Implementation (World Bank Technical Paper Number 88, 1988).

G. North American Free Trade Agreement

Price, Daniel M., *An Overview of the NAFTA Investment Chapter: Substantive Rules and Investor-State Dispute Settlement*, 27 The Int'l Lawyer 727 (1993).

Rugman, Alan M.(ed.), Foreign Investment and NAFTA (1994).

Twomey, Michael J., Multinational Corporations in the North American Free Trade Association (1993).

II. Host Country Investment Laws

A. Generally

Anthoine, Robert, ed., *Tax Incentives for Private Investment in Developing Countries* (1979).

Committee on Economic Development, *Transnational Corporations and Developing Countries: New Policies for a Changing World Economy* (1981).

Diamond, Walter H. and Dorothy B. Diamond, *Capital Formation and Investment Incentives Around the World* (2 vols. 1981, 1982).

International Centre for Settlement of Investment Disputes, *Investment Laws of the World: The Developing Nations* (multi-volume 1977, 1982).

Soloveytchik, Viktor. New Perspectives For Concession Agreements, 16 Hous. J. Int'l L. 261, 267 (1993).

Surrey, Walter Sterling and Don Wallace, Jr., eds., 4 *A Lawyer's Guide to International Business Transactions* (2d ed. 1980).

B. Eastern Europe

Bososiewicz, Zbigniew, *Foreign Investment in Eastern Europe* (1992).

Lorentzen, Jochen, *Opening Up Hungary to the World Market: External Constraints & Opportunities* (1995).

Paliwoda, Stanley J., *Investing in Eastern Europe: Opportunities Explored* (1993).

[See also listings under Joint Ventures, Eastern Europe, *infra.*]

C. European Economic Community

Dixon, John C., *Tolley's Trading in Europe: A Guide to Business and Taxation* (1992).

Everling, Ulrich, *The Right of Establishing in the Common Market* (CCH, 1964).

Hood, Neil and Stephen Young, *British Policy and Inward Direct Investment*, 15 J. World Trade L. 231 (1981).

Stein, Eric, *Harmonization of European Company Laws: National Reform and Transnational Coordination* (1971).

D. Japan

Eide, Tord. J., *How to establish Business in Japan: A Guide to Legal Issues Such as Taxation, Labor & Establishing Technicalities* (1991).

"Japan," in 4 *A Lawyer's Guide to International Business Transactions* (Walter Sterling Surrey and Don Wallace, Jr., eds. 2d ed. 1980).

Sckolnick, Lewis B. (ed.), *Japan: Trade, Licensing & Investing Rules and Regulations* (1994).

E. Latin America

American Bar Association, *Current Legal Aspects of Doing Business in Latin America* (S. Stairs ed. 1981).

Behrman, Jack N., *Decision Criteria for Foreign Direct Investment in Latin America* (Council of the Americas 1974).

Campbell, Dennis (ed.), *Legal Aspects of Doing Business in Latin America* (2 vols.) (1992).

Grosse, Robert E., *Foreign Investment Codes and the Location of Direct Investment* (1980).

Radway, Robert J., and Franklin T. Hoet-Linares, "Venezuela Revisited: Foreign Investment, Technology and Related Issues," 15 Vand. J. Transnat'l L. 1 (1982).

Reference Manual on Doing Business in Latin America (D. Shea, F. Swacker, R. Radway, S. Stairs, eds. 1979).

Rosenn, Keith S., *Foreign Investment in Brazil* (1991).

Southern Methodist University, *Doing Business in Mexico* (B. Carl ed. 2 vols. 1980–82).

F. Middle East

Abraham, Nicholas A., *Doing Business in Saudi Arabia* (1980).

Abraham, Nicholas A., *Doing Business in Egypt* (1979).

Carr, David W., *Foreign Investment and Development in Egypt* (1979).

Kay, Ernest, *Legal Aspects of Business in Saudi Arabia* (1979).

Salacuse, Jeswald W., "Egypt's New Law on Foreign Investment: The Framework for Economic Openness," 9 *Int'l Law.* 647 (1975).

Salacuse, Jeswald W., and Theodore Parnall, "Foreign Investment and Economic Openness in Egypt: Legal Problems and Legislative Adjustments of the First Three Years," 12 *Int'l Law.* 759 (1978).

G. People's Republic of China

Pattison, Joseph E., "China's Developing Framework for Foreign Investment: Experience and Expectations," 13 *Law & Pol'y Int'l Bus.* 89 (1981).

H. Other

Ho Il Yoon, "Legal Aspects of Foreign Investment in the Republic of Korea," 10 *Int'l Law.* 729 (1976).

Southwestern Legal Foundation, Private Investments and International Transactions in Asia and South Pacific Countries (1974, 1975).

III. Joint Ventures

A. Generally

Buffenstein, Daryl Rodney, "Foreign Investment Arbitration and Joint Ventures," 5 *N.C.J. Int'l L. & Com. Reg.* 191 (1980).

Comment, "Protecting the Entrepreneur: Special Drafting Concerns for the International Joint Venture Contracts," 14 *U.C.D. L. Rev.* 1001 (1981).

Hushon, John D., "Joint Ventures Between Multinationals: Government Regulatory Aspects," 6 *N.C.J. Int'l L. & Com. Reg.* 207 (1981).

King, Henry R., Jr., "A Case Study—Legal Considerations in the Formation and Operation of Foreign Joint Ventures: Brazil, European Communities (EEC), Japan and Andean Common Market (ANCOM)," 1979 *Tax Mgmt. Int'l J.* 79–12, 18 (1979).

The Multinational Joint Venture: Planning & Negotiating (New York Law Journal Seminar, H. Ravine ed. 1981).

Goldsweig, David B. & Roger H. Cummins, *International Joint Ventures: A Practical Approach to Working With Foreign Investors in the U.S. and Abroad* (1990).

Travaglini, Vincent D., "Foreign Licensing and Joint Venture Arrangements," 4 *N.C.J. Int'l L. & Com. Reg.* 159 (1979).

Vishny, Paul H., *Guide to International Operations* (1981).

B. Developing Countries

Friedman, Wolfgang G. and Jean-Pierre Beguin, *Joint International Business Ventures in Developing Countries* (1971).

Salacuse, Jeswald W., *Arab Capital and Trilateral Ventures in the Middle East: Is Three a Crowd?* in *Rich and Poor States in the Middle East* 129 (Kerr and Yassine, eds. 1982).

Shelp, R.K., *Dealing With Host Country Governments As Co-Venturers or Otherwise: How to Maximize the Good and Minimize the Bad or "How to Negotiate with Latin American Governments,"* in Current Legal Aspects of Doing Business in Latin America (S. Stairs ed. 1981).

Sunshine, Russell B., *Joint Ventures in Developing Countries,* in 2 Negotiating Foreign Investments: A Manual for the Third World 7.1B1 (R. Hellawell and D. Wallace, Jr. eds. 1982).

C. Eastern Europe

Campbell, Dennis, ed., *Legal Aspects of Joint Ventures in Eastern Europe* (1981).

Friedman W., ed., *Joint Business Ventures of Yugoslav Enterprises and Foreign Firms* (1968).

"Legal Aspects of East-West Joint Ventures," 10 *Int'l Bus. Law.* (April 1982).

Note, "Western Investment in State-Controlled Economies: Establishment of Joint Ventures in Eastern European Countries", 5 *N.C.J. Int'l & Com. Reg.* 507 (1980).

Scriven, John G., "Joint Venture Legislation in Eastern Europe: A Practical Guide," 21 *Harv. Int'l L.J.* 633 (1980).

Verzariu, Pompiliu, Jr. and Jay A. Burgess, *Joint Venture Agreements in Romania: Background for Implementation* (U.S. Department of Commerce, 1977).

D. Other Areas

Alford, William P., and David E. Birenbaum, *Ventures in the China Trade: An Analysis of China's Emerging Legal Framework for the Regulations of Foreign Investment*, 3 Nw. J. Int'l L. & Bus. 56 (1981).

Kryzda, B.F., *Joint Ventures and Technology Transfers*, 12 Case West. J. Int'l L. 549 (1980) [Latin America].

Shiao-Ming, S., *China's New Law on Joint Ventures Using Chinese and Foreign Investment*, 34 Sw. L.J. 1183 (1981).

IV. Forms of Business Organization

A. General

Commerce Clearing House, *Doing Business in Europe* (Chicago).

DeHoughton, C., ed., *The Company; Law Structure, and Reform in Eleven Countries* (1970).

Ernst & Ernst, *International Business Series* (New York).

Frommel, S.N. and J.H. Thompson, *Company Law in Europe* (1975).

Jones, Frank H., *One Thousand Questions and Answers on Company Law* (1975).

Lattin, Norman D., *The Law of Corporations* (1971).

Meinhardt, P., *Company Law in Europe* (1980).

Pennington, R.R., *Company Law* (1979).

Price Waterhouse, *Information Guides for Doing Business Outside the United States* (New York).

Zaphiriou, *European Business Law* (1970).

B. European Economic Community

Berger, D., "Harmonization of Company Law Under the Common Market Treaty," 4 *Creighton L. Rev.* 205 (1971).

Hood, J.B., "European Company Proposal," 19 *Int'l & Comp. L.Q.* 468 (1970).

Mann, F.A., "The European Company," 19 *Int'l & Comp. L.Q.* 468 (1970).

Ranier, D., "The Proposed Statute for a European Company," 10 *Tex. Int'l L.J.* 90 (1975).

Sanders, P., "European Company," 6 *Ga. J. Int'l & Comp. L.* 367 (1976).

Schmitthoff, C., ed., *The Harmonization of European Company Law* (1973).

Stein, E., *Harmonization of European Company Laws* (1971).

Stein, E., "Harmonization of European Company Laws," 37 *Law & Contemp. Probs.* 318 (1972).

Wriston, W.B., "The World Corporation: New Weight in an Old Balance," *N.Y. St. B.J.* 77 (1974).

C. By Country

1. Argentina

Bomchil, M., *Company Formation in Argentina* (1970).

2. Australia

Baxt, R., "Company Law and Securities," 9 *Austl. Bus. L. Rev.* 265 (1981).

Mason, H.H., *Australian Company Law* (1969).

Turnbull, S., *The Disadvantages of Australian Firms in Capital Creation* (1976).

3. Canada

DeBoo, R., *Canada Business Company Act and Regulations* (1976).

Dickerson, R. W. V. and D. L. Vaughan, "The Canada Business Corporations Act: Some Aspects of Transnational Interest," 8 *Vand. J. Transnat'l L.* 795 (1975).

Lapres, D., "Canada Development Corporation: A Proposal to Reconcile its Conflict of Objectives," 9 *J. Int'l L. & Econ.* 507 (1974).

Ziegel, J. S., *Studies in Canadian Company Law* (1967).

4. Caribbean

Surya, B. M., *The Harmonization of Caribbean Company Law* (1982).

5. China

Bosc, D.M., "The Law of the People's Republic of China on Joint Ventures Using Chinese and Foreign Investment," 6 *Brooklyn J. Int'l L.* i218 (1980).

Chang-Ching Huang, "The Law of China - Foreign Jointly Invested Operation Enterprise in the People's Republic of China," 85 *Comp. L. J.* 235 (1980).

Reynolds, P. D., "The Joint Venture Law of the People's Republic of China: Preliminary Observations," 14 *Int'l L.* 31 (1980).

Shen Shiao-Ming, "China's New Law on Joint Ventures Using Chinese and Foreign Investment," 35 *Sw. L.J.* 1183 (1981).

Topp, S. W., "Joint Ventures in the People's Republic of China," 14 *J. Int'l L. & Econ.* 133 (1980).

6. Eastern Europe

Gordon, M. W., "Joint Ventures in Eastern Europe," 9 *Tex. Int'l L.J.* 281 (1974).

Zoubek, J., "Joint Ventures in Eastern Europe," 9 *J. World Trade L.* 427 (1975).

7. England

Dalton, C., "Proposals for the Unification of Corporation Law Within the European Economic Community: Effect on the British Company," 7 *N.Y.U. J. Int'l L. & Pol.* 59 (1974).

Florence, P. S., Ownership, *Control and Success of Large Companies: An Analysis of English Industrial Structure and Policy 1936-1951* (1961).

Gower, L. C. B., *Company Law* (4th ed. 1979).

Gower, L. C. B., "Whither Company Law?"15 *U.B.C.L. Rev.* 385 (1981).

Griffith, R., "British Companies Operating in Hong Kong," 130 *New L.J.* 1157 (1980).

King, M. A., *Public Policy and the Corporation* (1977).

8. France

Catrice, R. L. and D. M. Scott, "Business Associations Under French Law," 120 *New L. J.* 590 (1970).

Church, E. M., *Business Associations Under French Law* (1960).

Elbow, M. H., *French Corporative Theory, 1889–1948* (1955).

Kozyris, P. J., "Equal Joint-Venture Corporations in France: Problems of Control and Resolution of Deadlocks," 17 *Am. J. Corp. L.* 503 (1969).

Rawlings, B. M., "French Company Law: Choice of Corporate Form Available to the Foreign Investor," 30 *Bus. Law* 1251 (1975).

9. Germany

Killius, *Business Operations in West Germany* (1975).

Kutschelis, G., "Doing Business in the Federal Republic of Germany," 3 *Den. J. Int'l L. & Pol.* 197 (1973).

Lutter, M., "Konzern in Germany Company Law," 1973 *J. Bus. L.* 278.

Lutter, M., "The German G.m.b.H. Law of 1980," 1981 *J. Bus. L.* 155.

Stratmann, G. H. W., "Partnerships v. Corporations: Why and When to Use Partnerships in the Light of Legal Format and Tax Treatment," 8 *Int'l Bus. Law* 317 (1980).

10. India

Encarnation, D. J., "The Political Economy of Indian Joint Industrial Ventures Abroad," 36 *Int'l Org.* 31 (1982).

Rungta, R. S., *The Rise of Business Companies in India, 1851–1900* (1970).

Tomlinson, J. W. C., *The Joint Venture Process in International Business: India and Pakistan* (1970).

11. Italy

Instituto Mobiliare Italiano, *Establishing a Business in Italy* (7th ed. 1969).

12. Japan

Hidebrand, J. L., "Establishing a Joint Venture Company in Japan: Legal Considerations," 6 *Case W. Res. J. Int'l L.* 199 (1974).

"Japanese Business Entities," 6 *Case W. Res. J. Int'l L.* 257 (1974).

Johnson, M. S., "Japanese Legal Milieu and its Relationship to Business," 13 *Am. Bus. L.J. 335* (1976).

Ross, S., "What is Japan, and What is not Japan?" 1980 *Bus. & Pol'y Rev.* 31.

Vaughan, R. T., "Introduction to Joint Venturing in Japan," 6 *Case W. Res. J. Int'l L.* 178 (1974).

13. Mexico

Gordon, M. W., "The Joint Venture as an Institution for Mexican Development: A Legislative History," 1978 *Ariz. St. L.J.* 173.

Hoagland, A. C., Jr., *Company Formation in Mexico* (2d ed. 1980).

14. Middle East

Nelson, R., ed., *Corporate Development in the Middle East* (1978).

15. Netherlands

Van De Ven, J. A., "Corporate Developments in the Netherlands", 27 *Bus. Law.* 873 (1972).

16. Nigeria

Onwuchekwa, G. M., "Doing Business in Nigeria," 128 *New L.J.* 215 (1978).

17. Norway

Arntzen, A., *Company, Trade and Tax Law in Norway* (1978).

18. Phillipines

Salonga, J.R., *Philippine Law on Private Corporations* (3d ed. 1968).

19. Singapore

Pillai, P. N., *Company Law - Singapore* (1979).

20. Soviet Union

Shillinglaw, T. L. & D. Stein, "Doing Business in the Soviet Union," 13 *Law & Pol'y Int'l Bus.* 1 (1981).

21. South Africa

Gibson, J. T. R., *South African Mercantile and Company Law* (1966).

22. Spain

Arroyo, I., "The One-Man Company in Spanish Law," 1981 *J. Bus. L.* 399.

23. Venezuela

Investment & Trade in Argentina, Brazil, Chile Mexico & Venezuela (Commercial Law and Practice Course Handbook, 1992).